FROM HIGH INCOME TO HIGH NET WORTH

DR. DAVID PHELPS, DDS

www.DavidPhelpsInternational.com

www.FreedomFounders.com

ABOUT THE AUTHOR
DR. DAVID PHELPS

AMERICA'S FREEDOM COACH

David owned and managed a private practice dental office for over twenty-one years. While still in dental school, he began his investment in real estate by joint-venturing with his father on their first rental property in 1980. Three years later, they sold the property, and David took his $25,000 capital gains share and leveraged it into thirty-one properties that later produced $15,000 net cash flow.

Multiple health crises suffered by his daughter, Jenna (leukemia, epilepsy and a liver transplant at age 12), caused David to leave practice, so that he could spend time with her.

Today, David is a nationally recognized speaker on creating freedom, building real businesses and investing in real estate. He also combines his professional and personal experiences to illustrate how the tactical and aspirational work together. David helps other logical, rational professionals become dreamers, then strategically manifest those dreams into freedom. He authors a monthly newsletter, "Path to Freedom" and hosts "The Dentist Freedom Blueprint" podcast. He is also the founder of the Freedom Founders Mastermind Community, providing the pathway to freedom for many professional practice owners.

"THE GREATEST RISK IN LIFE IS DOING NOTHING."

Dr. David Phelps

Learn more about David and book David to speak, at:
www.DavidPhelpsInternational.com

For More Information, Please Visit:

www.FreedomFounders.com

DEDICATION

This book is dedicated to my colleagues: the hard-working, over-achieving and under-appreciated dentists, doctors, and small business owners in this great country.
May you achieve your freedom.

PREFACE:
A Moment of Truth

This was never part of the original plan...

I had laid out my entire life in advance. "I've got this—the sky's the limit." Blessed with good intellect and a work ethic to boot. Failure was not an option. A perfect family. A perfect life. A perfect professional practice career. But there I was. Sitting on the small, vinyl, padded bench in Jenna's hospital room. The IV machine humming, holding several bags of fluids and meds, dripping into the tubes and through the needles that ran into her small and bruised hand. Jenna, only twelve years old, is asleep, her body still trying to recover from an exhaustive six hours of surgery removing her cirrhotic and failed liver and replacing it with the gift of life—a donor's liver. Away from my busy and stressful practice, I had a lot of time to think at that hospital. No cell phone access. Disconnected from the rest of the world, nothing else mattered. All of the daily "stuff" that had seemed so paramount wasn't even a blip on my radar. All of my education, wisdom, and experience; even all of the money I could earn—none of it mattered. None of it could make a difference. I could only hope. Hope and pray that Jenna would recover, and I would get a second chance. A second chance to be a father—a real father who would be present, not absent. Not preoccupied with "stuff." Would there be a "someday?" A day in the future when I could spend quality time with Jenna?

Time is never on our side. It marches on. There is a limited supply for each one of us. Tomorrow is not promised to anyone. Life is a gift. It was during Jenna's initial weeks of transplant recovery while spending day after day at Texas Children's Hospital in Houston, that I made a critical and life-changing decision. A moment of truth: **I would no longer practice dentistry.**

Creating a Plan B.

While a senior in college, I began reading books about investments. (I always had a knack for planning ahead.) I read books about stock market investing and some about real estate. Comparing the two, real estate won hands down. It was a tangible asset that I could control. Investing in the stock market made no sense to me. During my first year of dental school at Baylor College of Dentistry in Dallas (1980), I talked my dad into being my co-venture partner in acquiring a two-story brick rental house (an estate sale) in a solid Dallas neighborhood. We followed the fundamental rule of real estate: buy the worst house in a good Neighborhood. I learned how to manage this first asset for rental income. After graduation from Baylor in 1983, we sold the house and split about $50,000.00 in capital gains profit (capital gains are taxed at a much lower rate than ordinary, or active income). The epiphany for me was in realizing that I made a capital profit of $25,000.00 from this one real estate asset during the same period of time that I worked many, many hours as a waiter at night and on weekends with much less to show in net income. Why should I work for money all of my life when I could acquire good capital assets that would work for me whether I worked or not? I began to understand that if I could acquire enough assets, I wouldn't have to work as hard ... maybe not at all.

By continuing to purchase and invest in real estate, I was transitioning from working for money to investing money in capital assets that would produce cash flow, preserve and build wealth. This was my

"Plan B." Creating a Plan B was the key to my financial freedom. It was there when I needed/wanted it.

In 2004, with Jenna in the hospital, I decided to pull the trigger. Hard work, sacrifice and a disciplined approach to real estate investment, provided the foundation that allowed me to give up my good, but very restrictive career as a dentist. Not an easy decision, but I had a real "reason why."

Update on Jenna

Today, she is in college working towards an associates degree in occupational therapy. A published author, speaker... she's got the world by the short hairs. Pretty good for a kid who, at age sixteen, was reading and writing at a second-grade level. (She suffered through intense chemotherapy as a very young child to fight high-risk leukemia and suffered epileptic seizures from age eight to twelve.) She missed the first thirteen years of a "normal" kid's life. Courageous, driven, tenacious, a fighter. My girl.

Here's what I learned... Network or connections are the most important factor in orchestrating a secure financial future. It is also the most underutilized capital asset. Who you know is essential. Creating relationships is the hardest part of making real estate a viable investment and also the reason why so many novice investors fail. They try to do it all themselves. It takes time and work to establish these critical relationships. Many underestimate this crucial piece!

Why do you do what you do?

"David," other dentists ask me, "why aren't you retired?" What they mean is, "If you did so well with real estate and dentistry, why are you still going at it?" Fair question. It's true that I don't need to do ... anything, really. For me, I do what I do because it's the most significant way I can invest my time. A genuine passion for helping my colleagues break the chains from being slaves to their practices, their financial fears and helping them create freedom in their lives and the lives of their families -- this **is what** demands my attention. I love the fact that this gives me a platform and brings some of the best and brightest people in all areas of business, marketing, real estate, and finance, to Dallas four times a year. This community is my best insurance policy. With the volatility and unknowns in our economy and industry, bringing together a Board of Advisors allows us to stand apart from the fallout and find the opportunities that chaos brings. Being in the middle of all of the real estate opportunities within our group allows me to put deals together and help our members use various buckets of investment capital in the safest, most efficient, effective means possible.

Having the freedom to retire, and actually doing it, are worlds apart for me. I'll likely never retire in the typical sense. Remaining significant and relevant until my body and mind give out, now that sounds like a plan! My community and relationships give me the platform to do just that. What a gift!

Additional Resources From David:

1. **Listen to my weekly podcast:** "The Dentist Freedom Blueprint." Listen at: www.DentistFreedomBlueprint.com. It's where I connect with my Trusted Advisors and other industry Influencers to dig in deep, sifting and sorting strategies for growing wealth tax-free, crea-ting tax deferral compounding strategies, and building real net worth through sustainable passive cash flow.

2. **Check out my blog:** I post weekly quick-hitting videos and artic-les for those looking to jumpstart their freedom journey at www.FreedomFounders.com/Blog.

3. **Get Your Free Retirement Scorecard:** Benchmark your retire-ment and wealth-building against hundreds of other practice profes-sionals, and get personalized feedback on your biggest opportunities and leverage points. Go to www.FreedomFounders.com/Scorecard to take the 3- minute assessment and get your scorecard.

4. **Apply to visit Freedom Founders:** If you'd like to join dozens of dentists, docs, and practice professionals on the fast track to Free-dom (5-7 years max), visit www.freedomfounders.com/step-1 to apply for a seat.

FOREWORD

I was excited when I received the manuscript of this book to review. Private lending has created large amounts of wealth for many of my clients. Dealing with private money, as either the lender or the borrower, helped them grow their net worth so much faster and easier than if a bank had been involved. And private lending allowed them to survive "down" markets, when many people with bank financing go under.

Single-family houses remain one of the safest investments out there, and this book shows how individuals can participate in ways that best suit their interests and abilities, very often with tax-free (or almost tax-free) cash flow and appreciation.

This book also shines a spotlight on how government regulation and taxation are making it harder for an individual to create the wealth that will keep him or her from being dependent on government largess during retirement.

If you are still wondering whether government actions are going to affect you, your retirement and your wealth, read Chapters 1 through 12 closely. If you already "get it" and are ready to implement ways to build wealth, start at Chapter 13, read through to the end and go right to work on building your own custom solution.

The author who created this book doesn't make his living writing books. I know—I've been his personal CPA for almost forty years. Dr. David Phelps is a hard-working, insightful, experienced investor who is out there every day doing exactly what he teaches. I hope you enjoy and, most importantly, take action on the outstanding information in this book.

John Groom, CPA

AskJohnGroom.com

CONTENTS

Introduction: Your Road To Freedom 1

Note From The Author (2nd Edition) 8

1. Surviving and Thriving in the New Economy....................16

2. The Great American Wealth Transfer................................24

3. Active Vs. Passive Income 32

4. Investing on Main Street Instead of Wall Street...............38

5. Capital Assets – The Key To Your Future Freedom 44

6. What's Your Plan B? 54

7. Current Cash Flow Vs. Future Bank Equity 60

8. Why Real Estate? Why Now?...66

9. Why Single-Family Houses?...72

10. Equity And Debt Investments 82

11. Inflation – The Hidden Tax 88

12. Taxes – The No. 1 Enemy Of Wealth Building 94

13. Leverage – The Double-Edged Sword 98

14. Joint Ventures – The Key To Your Investment Success.....106

15. Managing Your Real Estate Investments – Or Not...........112

16. Due Dilligence Of The Joint Venture Partner 120

17. Due Dilligence Of The Property 126

18. Hard Money Lending - Investment Or Business? 134

19. High Cash Flow Yields - Performing Notes Secured........138

20. Back Door Real Estate Investment – Non-Performing Notes
    Secured By Real Estate...144

21. The Velocity of Money 150

22. What's a Fair Return on Investment 156

23. Documentation - Securing The Deal 162

24. What's the Downside Risk? 168

25. Are There Any Good Deals Left? 172

26. Your Investment Team 176

27. 401(K)s And Self-Directed IRAs, Health Savings Accounts
    and Coverdell Education Savings Accounts 180

28. Your New Plan For Building Wealth 186

29. Bonus Chapter: An Introduction To Syndications 192

30. Bonus Chapter: True Storys Of Financial Freedom 200

Appendix Article: Multiply Your Net Worth 206

INTRODUCTION

YOUR ROAD TO FREEDOM

If you are a dentist, self-employed and running your own professional practice, this book is for you.

America has always been a land of freedom, individualism and opportunity, not only for American citizens but for millions of immigrants who understand the value of the chance to get ahead in life.

Entrepreneurship and capitalism go hand in hand. The zeal for being one's own boss, to start a business, to create value and to exchange that value for money is what America is about.

The conundrum that every entrepreneur faces at some point is the over-focus on current income with the failure to build a model for creating one's future bank. Future bank is equity, net worth or real wealth that provides the basis for freedom and options (or the more traditional "retirement years"). Real wealth is the capital that we put to work on our behalf so that we don't have to work to create that income.

In the Freedom Founder's mastermind, we call this future bank wealth the pathway to freedom. Our client members, through my proprietary Freedom Blueprint™, determine their Freedom Number. Rather than an accumulation number (as set forth by the traditional financial models), the Freedom Number™ is a monthly cash flow number. It's the amount of money required before tax to provide the lifestyle overhead or "burn rate" of our client.

With an established Freedom Number, it becomes a simple math exercise to determine how much invested capital is required to produce the monthly cash flow that provides the security for the family needs (and wants). Invested in capital assets, the cash flow never depletes the original capital principal and instead provides a means to establish one's financial legacy and/or make significant charitable contributions.

It's a completely different (be forewarned, I am a contrarian, and a very successful contrarian) model that has life-changing implications for the hardworking entrepreneur and his family. Comments from our Freedom Founder's members are, "I only wish I had found you years ago!"

Too much authority is given to "outside advisors" to whom one's future financial plans are abdicated. Why? Because society and Wall Street have indoctrinated even the most wise and scholarly to believe that finances and financial planning are too complex for the untrained individual to manage.

My advice to those who have adopted this thinking is to only take long-term financial advice from someone who has already created the life to which you aspire. While each of us needs the very specific legal, tax and accounting advice of a lawyer or CPA.,the experience of an estate attorney or an insurance broker, none of these professionals has created the freedom lifestyle that you desire. Then why should you accept their advice, as well-meaning as it may be?

Once a business becomes successful through the hard work and efforts of its entrepreneurial owner, the next step is creating the transition plan to security and peace of mind. Owning and running a business provide the platform for achieving a certain lifestyle, true, but for most business owners that very success becomes the ball and chain that smothers them and keeps them from enjoying the fruits of their labor.

And then there's retirement. The prudent dentist, by earning and saving, has his or her sights set on a date when the practice can be sold and investment capital takes over, providing for the golden years.

But sometimes problems trip up even the best of us: maybe you don't make enough money to put into retirement savings; you started to save for retirement too late; you lost most of your retirement savings in the financial crisis; or you just don't trust the economy and government enough to stop working for a steady income.

But while most dentists have the goal of learning how to invest their money, not all have taken the time to learn how to maximize their investments.

Does that sound like you? What is your plan? Do you have a plan? Is your plan on schedule?

Don't feel badly if you don't like your answers. You are in good company; many dentists are in the same boat. The fact that you are reading this book is evidence that you are not satisfied with the status quo, or at least are curious to investigate another perspective.

There is a better way—a faster way—to reach that freedom point and provide options. Isn't freedom all about having options?

To learn more about how to give yourself and your family a bright financial future, keep reading.

A "Plan B" For Freedom

The traditional paradigms of investment and financial planning—that is, earning and saving one's way to retirement, followed by putting one's full faith and future in the hands of Wall Street (stock market or bonds)— are no longer valid, if they ever were.

Like it or not, today we live in uncharted waters, with political and economic dynamics that have never been experienced. Wall Street has not proven to be a good steward of our money. The outright manipulation, insider-trading and high-speed computerized functions of these markets are reason enough for them not to be the place for the prudent individual (retail) investor to place his or her hard-earned capital.

Historically, more wealth has been created via real estate than any other investment class. The majority of business owners who are financially free have a significant portion of their assets invested in real estate.

Recently, Warren Buffett said: "If it were practical to load up on single-family homes, I would." After the 2008 Great Recession, Warren Buffett is systematically buying up real estate brokerages throughout the nation, providing him access to all of the single-family properties that he desires.

Why not commercial or multi-family REITs (real estate investment trusts), PPMs (private placement equity funds), limited partnerships, or TIC (tenant-in-common) vehicles? Each of these investment classes allows for ease of investment for the passive investor who wishes to diversify into real estate, but they also come with a loss of control and more significant downside risk.

The problem with each of these asset classes is that the investor loses oversight over the investment. Capital is pooled with other investors, and a management entity (which generally takes a handsome fee on the front end plus management fees during the holding period) handles the administration and decision-making authority during the investment asset holding period. In an ideal world, the investor receives the anticipated return on investment also known as the "proforma return" plus his original capital invested (return of principal).

Unfortunately, the loss of investment control, simply in order to be passive, can result in a loss of investment capital. The Internet is full of news about lawsuits involving unhappy investors who believe they were misled, felt the management entity invested in inappropriate investments or mismanaged the assets, and so on.

So what are the options for the individual investor who is busy and focused on running and maintaining a viable business or professional practice, yet doesn't want to lose control over his or her investments by handing them over to Wall Street or by pooling investment capital with syndications? (See the chapter on Syndications to learn how to invest the "right way" in a syndication.)

Answer: Direct ownership assets. This implies 1 owner: 1 asset. In alternative investments, this would be single-family residential assets, both equity and debt.

Common objections or barriers for the novice single-family real estate investor are:

1. Inefficient market – it's not easy! (An "efficient" market is the stock market.)

2. Limited access to opportunities. (Where and how does one find "good deals"?)

3. No centralized management. (The investor's nightmare!)

4. Lack of liquidity. (It takes time to liquidate real estate equity.)

These objections to single-family investment are what make this asset class a prime opportunity for those who wish to build wealth in today's economy. We are now experiencing a massive transfer of wealth (redistribution).

Those who have access to and an understanding of local markets are taking advantage of acquiring these assets at well-below replacement cost and with cash flow returns well into double digits. Strict credit financing and underwriting regulations have reduced the number of homeowners who can qualify for financing, which in turn causes rents (cash flow) to increase.

The inefficiencies in the market—the fact that real estate values cannot be traded on an exchange—are what give the astute investor the real opportunities. These inefficiencies prevent real estate from being manipulated by high-speed computer or insider trading, and professional or sophisticated traders are kept out of the market.

Finding good deals is an art and requires both a local presence or network and the ability to lead-generate through various sources. The passive investor must rely on a co-venture partner who is a "boots-on-the-ground" active investor in order to gain access to the best opportunities. It's all about the connection, or "who you know."

Almost everyone has or knows someone who has a landlord/tenant horror story. But it is this very management skill that creates real opportunities for those who know how to either systematize or outsource the management component. Real estate investment is not for the person we call the "accidental landlord." Someone must set up management systems and processes.

The fast track for the passive investor to find the best local opportunities and handle the management issue is through purposely structured joint ventures with an active co-venture partner. A joint venture is not a partnership.

Joint ventures provide for severable (separate) interests in real estate that are documented and secured and do not require the future division of interests through litigation (the messy downside to traditional partnerships).

The most successful people in the world are those who learned early that almost any endeavor can be achieved more efficiently by collaborating with others who bring complementary assets, skills or resources to the project or investment. Going solo limits the efficiency and ability to achieve and produce more.

Real estate values have always been dependent on the availability of financing. When interest rates are low, and banks and mortgage institutions are providing relatively easy credit financing, real estate is more liquid and values increase. (This was the driving force in the housing bubble that peaked in 2006.)

During times of limited access to credit financing, housing values decrease and real estate is less liquid (the cause of the housing bubble collapse that began in 2007 and continued for another three to four years).

Novice investors consider traditional bank institutions the main source of investment financing. This limits the investor to the bank's lending criteria and requires placing all of one's personal assets at risk (personal liability). Experienced investors have long avoided bank financing for acquisition and holding periods, and instead utilize both private lenders and seller financing for leveraged acquisitions.

When one has developed access to private funds, no longer are real estate investments illiquid, and leverage financing carries much less risk. Additionally, private funds can be used in both equity and debt financing (the former being the most risk-averse form of financing).

NOTE FROM THE AUTHOR

HOW RESETS CREATE OPPORTUNITY

This second edition has been revised and updated three months (June 2020) into the coronavirus pandemic and subsequent government-mandated shutdown of all but "essential" business operations.

My belief and experience is that the words on the following pages are even more relevant during times of volatility and crisis than during times of economic expansion.

Why? Because people are more in tune with the vulnerability of having only a Plan A, which for all intents and purposes, has been altered significantly for the majority. They realize that the security they thought they had can be (and has been) severely disrupted. But your personal economic and financial situation does not have to mirror that of the rest of the country or the rest of the world...IF...you are not afraid to chart a course that does not follow the majority. Is that you? I hope so. I love being surrounded by those who are willing to embark on the road less travelled. This book will explain why a Plan B which provides for multiple streams of income NOT dependent on your work effort can propel you to your freedom destination more quickly and with much more

"Most of life's opportunities come out of moments of struggle"
- Ray Dalio

certainty than the traditional financial planning models that have failed.

The Great Reset 2.0 - How to Hit Your Next Inflection Point

The American standard of living, particularly in the last ten years, has been built on a house of cards - debt. Without the dollar being the world reserve currency, this would not have been possible.

A life, a business or a country cannot sustain itself indefinitely on debt. At some point, the payment is due.

The coronavirus outbreak was the trigger for an event (recession) that was overdue.

"If you know the enemy and know yourself, you need not fear the result of a hundred battles. If you know yourself but not the enemy, for every victory gained you will also suffer a defeat. If you know neither the enemy nor yourself, you will succumb in every battle."
— Sun Tzu, The Art of War

Change is inevitable. You can respond to it in one of two ways: You can embrace it, modify your investment strategy around it, and reap the benefits from the opportunities that present themselves. Or you can fear it, refuse to adapt, miss out on the opportunities that come your way, watch your profits shrink, and potentially lose wealth and money.

Market Cycles - Get Used to It

Market cycles are part of life. Since 1854, there have been 33 such cycles, the average length of time from peak to peak just over fifty-six months. Four cycles since 1960 have lasted nine years or more. The most recent economic expansion lasted 126 months until the coronavirus appeared out of nowhere.

Markets—including the real estate market—are made up of billions of transactions. Those markets comprise the overall economy. The economy goes up and down in cycles over the period of years and decades.

What do these cycles do to our long-term wealth and Freedom planning? (freedom doesn't have to mean retirement - it indicates options; choice). For most, they are very upsetting, tossing previous dreams and plans into the gutter. A re-start; a do-over.

Eventually, one runs out of time., leading to what Henry David Thoreau described as "men living lives of quiet desperation."

I would call it, "living lives of regret."

The Great Wealth Transfer

The coronavirus pandemic will be a defining moment for this nation for many years.

With every recessionary downturn, wealth is lost by the majority. Retirement plans, 401(k)'s and other traditional investment accounts lose value. On average, it takes another six to eight years for an individual to get back to even. How many market resets can you endure?

The next several years will involve painful deleveraging. More painful than in the past because of the massive debt that the world and the U.S. have accumulated.

With every recessionary downturn, wealth is lost by the majority. Retirement plans, 401(k)'s and other traditional investment accounts lose value. On average, it takes another six to eight years for an individual to get back to even. How many market resets can you endure?

Income is Not Wealth

If the amount of money you earn is limited by the number of hours you work, you will never be wealthy.

Capital assets (real businesses and real estate that produce annuity income independent of your labor) set you free. You move from working harder to working smarter by acquiring and increasing the value of those capital assets.

Society, parents and our education system focus our attention on learning to "do something." To get a job, begin a career, enter a profession. All emphasis is on "doing" - active income generation. Transactional.

Most small business owners wake up every day focused on one thing - current income with no thought of how fragile this leaves him without other revenue streams.

As long as you show up every day, you generate income. Stop working and so does the income. That's risky. The worst number in business is the number 1. It is fragile. Dependence on active income causes an abdication from creating real wealth. For most, that high income is nothing more than a high-paying job.

Equity matters - not just current income. Equity from the existing business and equity acquired or created outside the business.

The traditional financial models have no concrete answer. Ask a typical financial advisor and his advice is, "you can retire in practice." Yikes! That sounds like a cop-out if I ever heard one.

The best way that I know to create outside wealth and equity is through real estate - alternative investments. Substantial benefits exist with real estate investments not available through other financial products.

Most of the high net worth members of the Freedom Founders community don't talk about day trading, beating stock indexes or avoiding taxes or achieving the highest possible return on their investments. They have moved beyond those schemes.

What they seek is 1) preservation of capital, 2) recurring annuity cash flow tied to inflation and 3) the ability to pass on to their heirs, not just monetary wealth, but the ability and resourcefulness to create it in a highly volatile environment.

Our members value the other 4 Freedoms, the first being **financial**. Having **time** discretion, focusing on the most critical **relationships**, securing the best **health** possible, and finally, understanding and finding real **purpose and meaning** in their lives.

The Five Freedoms

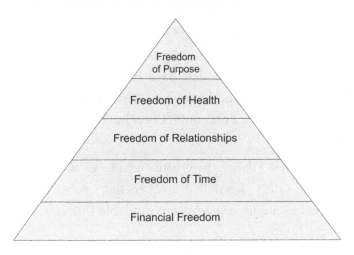

"There are two types of pain you will go through in life: the pain of discipline and the pain of regret. Discipline weighs ounces, while regret weighs tons."

Instead of owning the gift of time, time that can be devoted to family, legacy and philanthropy, the majority remain steadfast at the money income game and often miss the best opportunities in life.

Money is not the goal – it's the currency you use to achieve the goal. Until you realize that, you'll never feel settled. You'll never find freedom.

I truly hope that the following chapters open your eyes to an alternative path to Freedom that doesn't rely on big institutions, Wall Street, the government, or the conventional wisdom we've all been taught. My goal is to help you take control of your life so that you can experience the 5 Freedoms and live a fulfilling life of purpose. Remember, financial Freedom is just the beginning.

Here's to your freedom, to you and your loved ones, and to the legacy of the generations to follow.

Dr. David Phelps

www.FreedomFounders.com

(972) 203-6960

1 Surviving and Thriving in the New Economy

SO WHAT HAPPENED?

"Toto, I don't think we're in Kansas anymore." Dorothy, in the classic movie The Wizard of Oz, said it well. It's a new land, a new economy, a new playing field where all of the old rules are gone. As noted previously, this "new normal" and reset happens during every business cycle.

The problem for the majority of Americans is that they will continue to act, to work, to invest as if the old normal was still intact. This effort will be similar to paddling upstream—very hard to gain any ground and very easy to lose ground if the paddling isn't 100% efficient. Who can keep up that effort and for how long?

By having an even basic understanding of the fundamentals of our New Economy and the interventionist policies of our government and the Federal Reserve, people can begin to make decisions and plans that will have them paddling with the current.

Our government needs money—a lot of it. And it will continue to need more and more. That problem is not going to go away; in fact, it's only going to get worse.

The U.S. cannot balance its budget. Trillions of dollars have been added to the national debt since the 2008 financial meltdown, more than doubling all the debt accumulated in the first 237 years of our country's existence!

"Our government needs money — a lot of it. Our politicians know no spending limits"

The 2020 coronavirus pandemic-turned government shutdown and now recession has again caused a bailout "relief" in the form of trillions of additional dollars into the economy through the CARES Act legislation, the largest ever economic stimulus in our country's history.. The Federal Reserve and The Department of the Treasury came up with a scheme that, in effect, gives the Treasury to the Fed's printing press. As our currency is no longer tied to a gold-backed standard, our Federal Reserve is free to print (digitally) all the money that it desires. This "bandaid stimulus" is additional debt that kicks the debt-repayment problem to future generations.

Unfortunately, the merging of the Federal Reserve and the Treasury is likely going to cause more problems than it fixes (unintended consequences).. In effect, it gives the Fed more power, and will likely be used to allow the central government to purchase assets that the central government really shouldn't be owning -- like financial institutions and corporate equity.

What happens when a President (whether the current one, the next one or the one after that) wants to nationalize private industry? What happens when a President decides that the government needs to control housing...or manufacturing...or the financial sector...and then directs the Treasury to start buying up pieces of those industries and directs the Fed to pay for it? What has been the result of the government "takeover" of the healthcare industry?

This is a disaster to the foundation of capitalism on which our country was founded, not as a perfect economic system, but the best that the world has experienced. Thi is going to lead to further corruption and control of private industry by the central government (what some might call "socialism").

This gives essentially unfettered power to the President -- who will now have the ability to directly impact monetary decisions made by the Fed and purchasing decisions made by the Treasury.

Eventually the piper must be paid. Where does all this money go? During the recent economic downturn, much of it was hoarded by the banks, which can simply loan it back to the Federal Reserve on a set profit margin with absolutely no risk to the bank.

Because the banks are largely controlled by the government based on regulatory mechanisms largely enforced since the 2008 economic collapse, the banks have little incentive to be aggressive in loaning money to businesses and consumers. When the banks do make such loans, the underwriting process has become so stringent and daunting that few businesses and consumers have the capability or desire to go through the process.

Today, China, Japan and the Saudis own a lot of our country's debt. With the devaluation of our dollar currency because of Federal Reserve policies to print more money, eventually these foreign debt-holders will "call in their notes," meaning they will demand higher interest rates to compensate for the loss in buying power of the dollar.

Even a small hike in interest rates, a percentage point or two, will have devastating consequences to our economy. The only way that our government is getting away with the current monetary policies is because the Fed has been able to control interest rates—but that won't last for long. When rates go up, the interest payments on our ever-increasing national debt will suck more money out of the economy and require more money for a government that knows no limits.

Additionally, this massive increase in the money supply will eventually lead to hyperinflation. More money chasing the same amount of goods or services has the direct cause and effect of driving up prices (due to the devaluation of the dollar). Those on fixed incomes are the people most devastated by inflation, although everyone is affected. If you have been planning on needing a certain nest egg of investment capital on which you can someday retire, inflation will require that number to be much higher.

The more inflation, the greater the number you will need to have. Is there a way that you can offset the negative consequences of inflation? The answer is yes. But it's not by buying stocks, bonds, mutual funds or even gold and silver.

How does all of this really affect you and me? Consider our seniors, those 65 years and older who, for the most part, are no longer actively earning wages or operating businesses. Their "active" income has ceased, and they are dependent on retirement plans, Social Security and their own investment savings.

Most seniors are conservative investors, as they should be. Preservation of the corpus, or principal investment capital, is key. They are not in a position to make risky investments in which principal could be lost. Younger people have time to make up for such losses, but after age 62, time is of the essence.

Instead, seniors invest in low-risk investments such as bank certificates of deposit, savings accounts, money market accounts, etc. Earning less than 2% on such investments leaves little return to offset increases in the cost of living, health care and prescriptions. In essence, the monetary policies and fiscal irresponsibility of our government are causing great hardship for seniors at a time when they can least afford it.

There is a way that our seniors can be helped, and it is through the entrepreneurial activity of people just like you and me.

Traditional financial-investment planning did allow for savers to prosper by putting their money into relatively conservative investments such as savings accounts, money market accounts or bank CDs. Today, due to the manipulation of interest rates by the Federal Reserve, savers—the majority of whom are retirees and seniors—are in a serious dilemma. Returns on conservative investments are currently in the low single digits. After accounting for taxes and inflation, such a low return cannot provide the cash flow necessary to maintain the lifestyle of most. Many must invade the principal of their retirement investments, reduce their standard of living, and go back to work full or part time.

This was not the vision of the people in this hard-working generation when they thought they had planned and saved well. To their misfortune, they listened to well-meant advice from those who had relied on more-traditional economic and retirement models. Those models do not work today. Conservative saving and investment is simply not a viable plan.

Conservative saving and investment is simply not a viable plan.

Many financial planners tout the stock market, municipal bonds or insurance annuities. These investment vehicles have been the stronghold of traditional financial planners simply because that's what their education and training have taught them.

Buying, selling and trading these investment assets are easy from a mechanical standpoint because each market is what we call an efficient market, one in which the assets are easily priced or valued. The ability to buy and sell is fast and efficient, and information to evaluate these assets is widely known and available to the public.

In this efficient market, products trade easily and quickly and with minimal "friction" from trading costs, and there is enough volume that buyers and sellers are generally available. While that all sounds lovely, in such a market it is pretty hard to find a bargain. And, over the long run, it is nearly impossible to "beat the market." The investor is better off to simply "buy the market" and attempt to ride the average.

The convention of public markets since the crash in 1929 has been complete disclosure—everybody has access to the same information at exactly the same time. In such an environment it is difficult to get a competitive advantage over the other bidders, and everything becomes "fully priced" very quickly after new information is made public.

How about gold and silver or other precious metals, conventionally thought of as good inflation hedges? There very well could be a place in one's portfolio for this investment asset.

This asset class does provide a level of liquidity indexed to inflation; however, there are no cash flow or dividends produced. Where and how to store bullion or coins may also present a dilemma. Every investment class has pros and cons—purposeful diversification is the key.

CHAPTER KEY TAKEAWAYS

 The U.S. debt will have a major effect on retirement planning and goals.

 The potential for high inflation must be considered in one's investment asset allocation.

 Individual investors can only hope to ride the stock market and not beat it.

 Real estate provides both cash flow (dividends) plus a hedge against future inflation.

NOTES

_____

_____

_____

_____

_____

_____

_____

_____

_____

PLAN OF ACTION

_____

_____

_____

_____

_____

_____

2 THE GREAT AMERICAN WEALTH TRANSFER

WHEN THE FINANCIAL, credit and housing collapse and crisis occurred in 2008, the government came to the rescue—with trillions of dollars of our taxpayer money. Almost 12 years later, the government once again spent trillions of dollars propping up the economy during the unprecedented global shutdown caused by the COVID-19 pandemic. I don't disagree that some level of intervention was necessary to prevent an all-out collapse and perhaps events similar to the Great Depression. But the future consequences of these decisions must not be underestimated.

In an economic downturn or recession, wealth is never destroyed—it merely changes hands.

During the first two years of the nation's "economic recovery," post 2008, the mean net worth of households in the upper 7% rose by approximately 28%, while the mean net worth of households in the lower 93% dropped by 4%.

How do the rich get richer and the poor get poorer?

The majority of households are dependent on the active income of wages and salaries or self-employed income. For most, their largest investment is usually a home (a home is actually a liability, but for the sake of this example we will call it an asset).

The upper 7%, on the other hand, are often heavily invested in other assets. Their home is usually only a fraction of their wealth.

93% of households lost millions in their homes and many lost their jobs. The wealthy also lost equity in their homes, but by being a small percentage of their asset base, that loss was relatively inconsequential.

It is a fact that more millionaires are created during times of economic recession or depression than in prosperous times.

Not dependent on a job for income, the wealthy were able to hang on and ride the subsequent Wall Street recovery (thanks to the trillion-dollar taxpayer bailout) and increase their wealth by 24 times more than the bottom 93% of households.

It is a fact that more millionaires are created during times of economic recession or depression than in prosperous times. Those who have positioned themselves strategically to not be dependent on an active income are able to leverage the opportunities created in the marketplace by the chaos and turbulence.

Here is what is happening now: With the Federal Reserve artificially holding interest rates at historic lows and Congress pumping massive stimulus money into the economy, the markets are being artificially propped up but with little foundation underneath. The newfound money has to go somewhere. Wall Street primarily goes into the stock market, but investors also understand the value play in real estate.

Post-2008, real estate was on sale in America. The collapse in 2008 stripped the equity from homeowner and investor alike; foreclosures and mortgage defaults spent years in the pipeline and working out back into the marketplace. There were numerous opportunities for investors with access to buy assets at steep discounts. It was a buyer's market.

For the next 10+ years, valuations rose steadily until the markets again reached a euphoric high. These gains lured large numbers of fairweather investors into the real estate marketplace. Encouraged by glamorized HGTV success stories and an army of self-fashioned real estate "experts," many entered the real estate market even as we reached historic highs.

The 2020 recession (caused by the global shutdown in response to the COVID pandemic) brought a reality check to many of these fairweather investors. What does that entail for the future?

I'm not an advocate of significant investment in the stock market (see my introduction), so I will concentrate instead on the history and future of the housing market. Hedge funds, which historically invest in the financial markets, have begun to eye market recessions as an opportunity to invest in real estate.

These funds are bringing billions of dollars into major U.S. metropolitan areas and snapping up foreclosed properties, and at the same time increasing values in those markets. In fact, more than 60% of all residential real estate in 2012 and into 2013 was purchased by cash buyers (aka investors and hedge funds).

What this means is that the "recovery" in housing (post-2008) was not organic. A real recovery would mean that individual home buyers, especially first-time buyers, would be entering the market and increasing house prices. This is not happening, and therefore the post 2008 recovery is not real and not sustainable (similar to the stock market).

In addition, the massive disruption caused by the 2020 pandemic shutdown promises to create significant opportunity (much like the aftermath of 2008) for investors with liquidity and access to acquire assets on sale.

What does this mean for you? If you learn how to access and invest in the real estate market, safely and with limited risk, you too can ride the wave of the money supply.

Unlike the stock market, real estate produces cash flow, regardless of valuation. Yes, there is a management component, but in Chapter 15 we'll cover how you can handle that without involving your time.

Simply understand that your taxpayer money is being pumped back into the market into assets that can be acquired today at very low prices—in fact, it's the best time in the past 40 years to be investing in real estate.

When purchased using the principles discussed in this book, real estate provides cash flow and an inflation index. (Remember our discussion of inflation?) There are also tax advantages and the availability of using safe leverage to multiply your wealth-building.

If this is true, you might ask, then why don't more people invest in real estate? Or, why doesn't my financial planner/adviser recommend real estate? Let's take the second half of the question first.

Most financial advisers are not trained or versed in the fundamentals of real estate investing. Their training is in financial assets such as stocks, bonds, mutual funds and insurance products. By recommending these investments, the adviser earns his or her living.

We're not saying there's not a place for a good financial adviser, but you should know what that place might be. A person will not and should not give advice on areas in which he or she has little or no experience and cannot be compensated.

The reason that more individuals don't invest in real estate is because real estate is an inefficient market. That means a person cannot simply go online and buy shares of a single-family property. (We should qualify that by mentioning real estate investment trusts, which do offer the ability to pool money into a fund or the like that invests in different classes of real estate—but we don't recommend that for you.)

Real estate markets are local and cannot be controlled or sold on an index like the Dow Jones or Nasdaq. Neither can the price or value of a single property be determined in seconds like shares of stocks, bonds or even gold.

If it's inefficient and not easy, then maybe there is an opportunity? Exactly. When something is not easy to do, that means the majority of the population will not do it and will look for the easier way.

Investing in real estate does require study and a knowledge of local markets, financing and management. The good news is that none of us has to become absolute experts in any of these areas in order to gain access to and prosper through the benefits of real estate investing. Interested? Keep reading.

CHAPTER KEY TAKEAWAYS

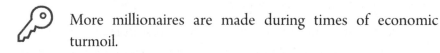

More millionaires are made during times of economic turmoil.

Real estate is "on sale" (a real bargain) today in America.

Most financial advisers don't understand and can't make a living recommending real estate as an investment.

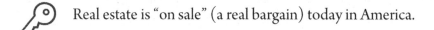

Real estate is an inefficient market and cannot be controlled or manipulated by high-speed institutional insider trading.

NOTES

_____

_____

_____

_____

_____

_____

_____

_____

_____

PLAN OF ACTION

_____

_____

_____

_____

_____

_____

Active Vs. Passive Income

WHY DOES IT matter, active or passive, if it's all income to you in the end?

What's the difference between active and passive income?

Active income is income received for services performed. This includes wages, tips, salaries and commissions, and income from businesses in which the owner has a material and active participation.

Active income is what is taught in school: Get good grades, earn scholarships, attain the highest degree possible so you can enter a career or start a business or professional practice that will allow you to earn a good living by active participation. In short, active income is simply "trading time for dollars."

And so it goes. With a strong work ethic, this model can produce a good standard of living for most. Then what's the problem? The problem is there's no freedom—no freedom in the sense of being able to take time off when desired to spend with the family or on hobbies or travel. Or, perhaps time to work on one's business or businesses.

Real freedom is doing what one wants to do, when he or she wants to do it, and with whom he or she wishes to do it. Selfish? Not necessarily.

Having freedom also means having the ability to help more people, whether through employment opportunities in one's business or by charitable giving of time and money to charities, missions or other causes.

Active income is where we all start. There is a sacrifice period during which we have more time than money. We work for money to provide the necessities and, later, the comforts of our chosen lifestyle.

Unfortunately for most, this is where it stops. It's our culture, our mindset, what we've been taught: work hard, provide good service and product, put money into savings, and everything will take care of itself.

The better way would be an evolving model. Yes, become educated, begin a career, business or professional practice, work hard, save some money, but as soon as possible, begin the transformation from working for money to having money work for you—24 hours a day, 7 days a week—whether you work or not. That's the strategy for real freedom.

Great! Then why doesn't it work for most? To find the answer, refer back to the traditional model of earning and saving for a lifetime using conventional financial models. In the end, they fail 96% of the population.

That's right! Over every demographic, regardless of the income earned throughout a lifetime, at age 65 only 4% of the population is able to retire and maintain the lifestyle desired; many find themselves having to remain in the active work-force for many more years than anticipated, often well into their 70s. Again, it makes no difference how much money was earned during the "working years."

This book is about how you, the active business or professional practice owner, can make the conversion from active to passive income. That's the real game. The sooner you get there, the sooner you have freedom!

Now that we've defined active income, what is passive income? This is income derived from rental property, interest, dividends, royalties, limited partnership interests or any other investment in which the investor is not actively involved.

Active income means you are actively involved in doing something in order to receive that income. Passive income means you are receiving that income with little or no effort or time in order to receive it.

Active income means you are actively involved in doing something in order to receive that income. It is not a hands-off participation. Some amount of energy and time must be expended in order to receive that income.

Passive income means you are receiving that income with little or no effort or time. For the most part, you are hands-off.

Reliance on active income, which we have already deemed as the norm for our country, does not provide freedom as defined. Passive income not only provides for freedom and options, it also is a form of insurance, security and peace of mind. If the majority of your income is solely dependent on your own labor efforts, what happens if something happens to you?

What if you are involved in a debilitating accident, develop a disability or chronic illness, or die unexpectedly? Yes, insurance is available to provide baseline assistance, but having passive income that you have created would provide so much more for you and your family should such an event occur.

What is the best way to create passive income? How does one do that while earning an active income, raising a family and creating a lifestyle? Is it all work and no play?

This is where investment in capital assets—well-located and safely financed real estate—comes in. We've already discussed the advantages of capital asset investment and how leveraging those investments can relatively quickly build both equity (net worth) and cash flow indexed to inflation.

What we haven't yet discussed is how you find the best and most suitable properties without becoming actively involved (unless your goal is to be an active participant). We'll handle those details in Chapter 14. Follow the path, and soon it will all make sense.

CHAPTER KEY TAKEAWAYS

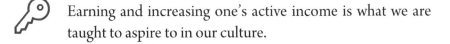

Earning and increasing one's active income is what we are taught to aspire to in our culture.

Passive income is most commonly equated with investing in paper or financial investments such as stocks and bonds. Real estate is not as well understood by the majority.

To reach financial freedom, one must convert from active to passive income through the acquisition of capital assets.

The ideal capital asset is real estate.

NOTES

_____

_____

_____

_____

_____

_____

_____

_____

_____

_____

PLAN OF ACTION

_____

_____

_____

_____

_____

_____

4 INVESTING ON MAIN STREET INSTEAD OF WALL STREET

WHAT ABOUT THE different financial investment classes?

There's an old saying in poker: "If you don't know who the sucker is at the table, it is you."

While money can be made in financial assets (stocks, bonds and annuities), it is a game for sophisticated players with connections in high places. The institutional investors (mutual funds and hedge funds) have trained professionals who invest for a living. They have experience and resources not available outside of their realm.

Sure, the Internet makes it seem like anyone can invest and trade like the pros, but that is not the case. The pros can control the momentum of a stock with their buy orders alone.

In addition, the pros have access to company CEOs and other executives, providing them information not available to the public. The ability to manipulate the market and profit with high-speed trading simply leaves the individual (retail) investor holding the bag.

Essentially, the market is rigged against the small investor, who is at an incredible disadvantage. It is not a fair market or level playing field.

What About Bonds?

Many who consider the stock market risky (and with good reason) have looked to bonds, or debt instruments, as a safer way to invest. Unfortunately, even bonds can create losses in one's portfolio.

Many who consider the stock market risky have looked to bonds.

Bond values also are artificially influenced by the Federal Reserve, which is buying U.S. bonds (debt) to the tune of $85 billion per month. Once the Fed retracts even slightly on this subsidization, the bond market (and stock market) will begin to head south, most likely rapidly.

With the Federal Reserve artificially holding interest rates at historic lows, the bond market is simply not producing the returns that might occur in normal markets. As interest rates rise (and they will), bond values will fall. Since interest rates can only go up, bonds are not an attractive investment class, especially not in the long term, which is where the better returns can be found today.

Municipal bonds are exempt from federal tax, which can provide greater after-tax returns than taxable Treasuries and other bonds. The problem today is that many municipalities are in financial trouble, thus making the face yield rate on these bonds a potentially riskier investment. Witness what recently happened in the Detroit bankruptcy. Many other cities are right behind Detroit.

Finally, bonds are vulnerable to inflation. Fixed-rate-return investments lose value, especially at lower rates of return, when the purchasing power of the dollar diminishes. Warren Buffett agrees that in the current economy, bonds are not a good play.

Annuities: Good or Bad?

Annuities are really not an investment, though many advisers sell them as such. An annuity is simply a contract between a person and a company. The person gives the company a sum of money and, in return, is promised a monthly payout, generally for the rest of his or her life.

Some examples may exist where annuities would make sense for retirees or folks planning to retire soon. At the same time, there are risks and situations where annuities may be the wrong choice.

With an annuity you essentially are paying a middleman, the insurance company, to invest in mutual funds and stocks on your behalf and then pay you a lower, albeit guaranteed, monthly income. You would do better accessing those investments yourself or paying a professional money manager. However, you should also consider why you would be in the stock market in the first place.

Finally, consider this about annuities: Have you ever heard of a hedge fund investing in an annuity? No. So, if the smart money isn't investing in annuities, maybe the average Joe retail investor should take the hint. Again, an annuity is not an investment; it is a contract.

Gold and Other Precious Metals

Precious metals will always have some value and certainly can have a place in a diversified investment portfolio. Gold, silver and other selected metals will remain steady in value if and when the government devalues the currency (inflation of the monetary supply or a complete currency crisis). However, they are not a source of passive income, as they do not provide any dividends or cash flow.

If the dollar disappears, you'll preserve the value of your wealth with precious metals. Generally speaking, precious metals neither depreciate or appreciate—they simply hold or maintain purchasing power. Five or ten percent of one's total investment portfolio in precious metals would be considered a prudent level of protection.

The topic of precious metals is beyond the scope of this book. It's not a bad idea to own some; just don't overdo it.

This short primer on the basic financial investments is by no means meant to be comprehensive and provide the reader with categorical information that should be used in definitive investment planning. There may be viable reasons to include any or all of the aforementioned classes in an overall strategy with diversification in mind.

CHAPTER KEY TAKEAWAYS

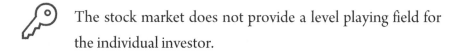

The stock market does not provide a level playing field for the individual investor.

Warren Buffett is not an advocate for bonds in an economy with pent-up inflationary factors.

Annuities are contracts, not investments.

Gold and precious metals generally provide a hedge against inflation, but do not provide any cash flow dividends.

NOTES

_____

_____

_____

_____

_____

_____

_____

_____

_____

PLAN OF ACTION

_____

_____

_____

_____

_____

_____

5 Capital Assets – The Key To Your Future Freedom

WHAT IS A capital asset? A capital asset is tangible property that cannot easily be converted to cash (as opposed to financial assets like stocks and bonds) and usually is held for a period of time as an investment; examples are businesses, real estate and equipment. A capital asset has intrinsic value due to its utility (use).

Capital assets have low correlations to stocks and bonds, so they are a good choice to lower one's overall portfolio risk while enhancing the potential for higher long-term, risk-adjusted returns. Capital assets help protect an investment portfolio against inflation because they represent the value of goods and services and NOT the value of a currency (as do financial assets like stocks and bonds).

Capital is what sets us free. Capital, particularly capital assets acquired for investment (vs. owning a home), provides clear-cut advantages and a pathway to freedom.

With a disciplined blueprint and principled strategies, real estate has historically been the best-known wealth-producing investment asset.

> *Because of the intrinsic value of capital assets and real estate, the acquisition of real estate can be leveraged.*

Because of the intrinsic value of capital assets and real estate, the acquisition of real estate can be leveraged, meaning that one does not have to save 100% of the purchase price of such an asset before being able to acquire it. This is unique to capital assets.

Leverage can be both good and bad. Properly used (more on that later), leverage is a tool that can allow for the multiplying effect of a good investment asset. This concept is not available for the other investment asset classes previously discussed.

For example, if I should desire to acquire a single-family rental property with a purchase price of $100,000, there are two basic ways for me to do it:

Plan#1:

I can save my money, perhaps $10,000 per year for 10 years, and then purchase the investment house. The problem is that the value of the house will likely go up over 10 years' time (due to currency devaluation and inflation), so after 10 years, I might need $150,000 to acquire the same house.

See the problem? By waiting until I have enough money saved for the purchase of a capital investment, the value may rise faster than my ability to accumulate the cash to buy it. I never get into the game!

Plan#2:

I use the $10,000 I've saved as the down payment and borrow the other $90,000 (90%) of the asset price on terms that still allow for a positive return on my cash invested ($10,000) after my debt service to the lender, management, maintenance and other associated expenses (which will be covered in detail in Chapter 15).

In the second example, not only was I able to acquire the real estate asset much earlier than if I had waited to save 100% of the purchase price, but I was able to control the asset (by owning it) with only 10% of my own money. Now when the value of this asset goes up because of inflation, I am "in the game" because I control the value, even though I am 90% leveraged. In addition, my cash flow (rents) will go up in tandem with inflation.

Let's go back to our original example. If I have to save 100% of the purchase price of one residential property, it might take me 15 years (factoring in the inflation index). Now that I own that one property it is debt-free, so all of the net income that is derived from that asset is direct net cash flow.

A $100,000 (now $150,000) asset might have a gross scheduled rent of $1,350 per month and net (after all expenses) of $810 per month. Annually, the net income would be $9,720, which would be a 6.5% return on the total cash investment of $150,000.

Continuing this program, with the additional cash flow from my now free-and-clear capital asset, I likely could purchase another similar house in almost half the time, maybe eight years. Continuing on, I could probably purchase a third such asset in about four more years, a fourth asset in two more years and, if desired, one new capital asset every year thereafter.

Of course, all of my "passive rental income" is going toward accumulation of assets. Eventually, I will want to stop accumulating and begin reaping the cash flow from these assets.

In summary, with Plan #1 I could acquire five single-family assets over 30 years with a total investment out-of-pocket of $300,000 (30 years times $10,000 per year). The additional capital came from the net rental cash flow from each property acquired during the acquisition period.

Factoring in inflation at 5% per year, those five rental-property assets would be valued at $1,246,000 and be producing a total of $2,800 per month net income per asset, or a total of $33,678 per year per asset and a combined annual net income of $168,393! That's a pretty respectable return on a $300,000 investment, yes?

OK, this was a simplified example in order to make a point. You may or may not agree with my use of a 5% inflation rate over 30 years. You may or may not agree with my use of a 40% expense ratio for each property. The point is, these five capital assets will produce a stable and regular cash flow and maintain that cash flow and asset value in an inflationary environment.

We have not yet discussed management, repairs, maintenance and capital improvements. I am not ignoring those items; they are definitely real and must be acknowledged and handled. Hold on, because we will get there.

While Plan #1 does work, the problem is that it took 30 years to acquire five primary capital assets that produce income by their intrinsic value and utility, the essential premise for investing in capital assets such as real estate.

If we go back to Plan #2, the leverage model, we can begin acquiring these same capital asset rental properties in year one instead of waiting 15 years to amass all of the necessary capital to acquire the first asset.

Let's see what that does for our model, using the same variables for inflation and expense ratios that were used in Plan #1. Our first house is acquired with just one year's savings of $10,000. The remaining $90,000 is borrowed via leverage (we'll talk later about leverage and where such financing is available).

For the purpose of this example, let's assume we obtain financing at 5% interest amortized over 30 years; that leaves a monthly debt service payment of $483. Subtracting that from our net income (Plan #1) of $810 per month leaves a remaining net cash flow of $327 per month or $3,922 per year, which equals a 39% return on the actual cash invested ($10,000).

The interesting aspect of investing in income-producing rental real estate is that the tenant-occupant pays down the debt.

So, the leverage of utilizing the capital asset (the rental property) to get what we needed (a 90% loan), that in turn gets us wh
perty), provided the ability to acquire the asset and produced a 39% return on our original $10,000 cash investment.

Remember, too, that we now control this capital asset so that we are in the game with inflation. (Since we control this property, the value and the rental cash flow will remain indexed to inflation.)

In year 2, we do the same thing. We take another $10,000 of savings (less the $3,922 in net rental cash flow from our first property acquisition) and purchase the second capital asset at $105,000 (remember 5% inflation) with a down payment of $10,500, or 10%.

You get the picture. Plan #2 allows us to purchase a single-family house investment asset every year instead of waiting 15 years to begin the acquisition. What does this plan do for our investment and wealth-building portfolio? In 15 years we own and control 15 properties with varying amounts of equity (i.e., the current market value of the asset minus the balance of any debt).

The property purchased in year 1, using the 5% inflation factor, would be valued at $208,000 and would, after 15 years, have a balance owed on the loan of $61,000, so the net equity of this property at year 15 would be $208,000 minus the $61,000 loan balance, or $147,000!

The cash flow, which began in year 1 at $327 per month, has also increased by the same annual inflation rate of 5% per year and is now a gross monthly rent of $2,800 and a net after expenses of $1,680, less the debt service principal and interest payment of $483, leaving a net cash flow of $1,200 per month!

Additionally, at year 15 we own a total of 15 rental properties, with a stair-step of cash flow and equity ranging from the property acquired in year 1 of $147,000 equity and $1,200 monthly cash flow, to the property just acquired in year 15, with a net equity of 10% of the current value of $208,000, or $20,800 and net monthly cash flow of approximately $680 per month.

The point is that by leveraging the acquisition of one new property each year, by year 15 the total investment portfolio net equity value and net cash flow value is at least a factor of 15 greater than the Plan #1 program, and no more out-of-pocket cash was required in the acquisition of the portfolio of 15 properties than in Plan #1, where the entire $150,000 purchase price had to be saved over 15 years.

It's the magic of leverage and one of the keys that savvy investors in real estate have used over and over again to build wealth and cash flow.

The interesting aspect of investing in income-producing rental real estate is that the tenant-occupant, through the value of the use of the property as living quarters, pays down the debt; pays for the expenses of maintaining the property, taxes and insurance; and provides the cash flow. All we had to do was come up with 10% of the total value of the property in order to acquire it.

We have used relatively simple examples to illustrate the advantages of leverage, a powerful concept only available for the acquisition of capital assets, simply because of their intrinsic value and utility. The proper and safe use of leverage will be covered in later chapters. Unsafe and speculative use of leverage has been the downfall of investors who failed to use principled investing.

CHAPTER KEY TAKEAWAYS

 A capital asset has intrinsic value due to its utility (use).

Capital assets protect against inflation because they represent the value of goods and services—not the value of a currency.

Leverage is the key factor for building wealth if used properly.

Leverage financing through the use of institutional debt is not advised for investment property acquisition.

NOTES

_____

_____

_____

_____

_____

_____

_____

_____

_____

PLAN OF ACTION

_____

_____

_____

_____

_____

_____

6 What's Your Plan B?

A PLAN B is a backup plan, ready to go, ready to implement when you want it or need it. The methodical and formulaic investment in real estate-secured assets has historically produced more wealth than any other asset class.

Once the investor-entrepreneur has reached the point where his or her passive income from the acquisition of capital assets (real estate) meets or exceeds the income produced by that person's own labor, financial freedom has been achieved.

Should something occur in a person's life that temporarily or permanently discontinues the ability or even desire to trade time for dollars (labor), reaching a point of financial freedom removes all of the stress and provides options.

Most Americans believe life is about getting a good education, which leads to a good job, career or profession and an appropriate lifestyle, then at age 62 or 65 they retire and live out the golden retirement years. Does it have to be this way? Who says?

These are simply ideas or a mindset implanted in our subconscious from an early age, and we simply believe "that is the way it is."

Only a small percentage of true entrepreneurs break that mold, understanding the principles of financial leverage and passive income streams from capital assets. They build freedom and wealth far beyond that of the average American. Is it luck? Good fortune?

> *The fact is, few Americans ever reach true financial freedom.*

I submit that those who find financial freedom early in life are no smarter and do not work any harder than other self-employed or career-minded people. They simply work smarter and without the baggage of a mindset that encourages hard work but not the building of real capital wealth.

The fact is, few Americans ever reach true financial freedom. Less than 5% of our population at age 65 can continue to live the lifestyle they have become accustomed to without some form of third-party assistance (Social Security, Medicare or other forms of government assistance).

Another 15% will be able to maintain a moderate lifestyle past age 65, as long as the aforementioned third-party assistance programs remain intact. The remaining 80% of people age 65 either must reduce their lifestyle once active work ceases or continue to labor for years longer in an attempt to maintain a certain level of lifestyle.

There is a sacrifice period that each of us must endure (unless one is the beneficiary of a large inheritance or trust fund), during which time we do exchange our labor for income. The point is, the majority will continue to rely on their labor and rising wages or salary to produce a desired or "entitled" lifestyle, often living at 100% plus of their net earnings (living on credit).

For the few who do have the discipline to fund excess or saved earnings, these funds typically go into a traditional "earn and save" 401(k), savings, CDs, or stock or bond mutual funds. These are what are known as financial asset accounts. These accounts typically are what financial planners or advisers sell clients simply because these strategies are what their education and training have told them is the right way and that is how they are paid—on commissions or fees—and not on results.

Anyone see a problem with this formula? It's all based on an old mindset of work hard, save, and "someday" you will be able to retire. This is the myth that I will dispel in this book.

How long should the sacrifice period be? That, of course, depends. It depends on a person's discipline over the lifestyle expectations agreed upon with his or her family. If there's no family at this point, those decisions are easy to make.

How much time beyond the person's active work (trading time for dollars) can be allocated toward capital asset acquisition? Will this person be more active in his investment activity because he has more time than money? Or can he earn more from his active work than by finding and managing capital assets? In that case, he might be a more passive, or at least a semi-active, investor.

Either option will work if the entrepreneur, active or passive, has a blueprint and formulaic schedule. The person also should be building and maintaining active relationship capital—the other people in his network who complement his active or passive engagement into capital asset investment.

The world needs active managers, and it needs passive investors. By surrounding oneself with capable people and being in the midst of this "investment activity," a person can quickly build assets to re-place his active income and surpass the sacrifice period.

Caution:

Do not attempt to do this by trying to find, negotiate, manage and fund each and every real estate property. This model will work, but it likely will take two, three or even four times longer than combining resources and assets with others in joint venture models where each person has a defined participation.

As a result, more deals are done with less effort. That is the key to wealth-building and a form of leverage. Don't miss this concept. It is very important in wealth creation and ultimate freedom.

CHAPTER KEY TAKEAWAYS

 Plan B is your back-up financial plan, providing freedom and options.

 Less than 5% of our population can retire without some form of third-party assistance.

 There is a sacrifice period in every person's life—you can control how long the sacrifice lasts and whether it occurs at a younger age or continues throughout your life.

 Leveraging other's time, skills and assets is a key to a viable financial freedom blueprint.

NOTES

_____

_____

_____

_____

_____

_____

_____

_____

_____

PLAN OF ACTION

_____

_____

_____

_____

_____

_____

7   Current Cash Flow Vs. Future Bank Equity

CASH FLOW IS our lifeblood. We are taught by parents, teachers and neighbors that the cash flow income needed to pay for lifestyle overhead is produced by the efforts of our labor. The higher the education, the better the career opportunities and, most likely, the better the cash flow.

Our current freedom is based on an equation whereby the income we produce by the efforts of our labor should exceed our lifestyle overhead. Unfortunately, the reverse is more often the case.

People go to school to get the education to get a job, go into a business or professional practice, and quickly find that ours is a credit-based society that rewards those who work hard with access to credit, allowing a person to live it up today and pay for it tomorrow.

This is a formula for failure. Yet many believe in it because these are the messages we receive. Besides, everyone else lives the big life with the big house, nice cars, vacations and private school. We deserve it! Don't we?

Fast forward to ages 62 or 65, society's definition of retirement age. To most, that should be the point of freedom. Work hard and then retire—but to what? And to what lifestyle? Health problems, disabilities, even the passing of a loved one can quickly vanquish the dream of the golden years.

Many are delaying retirement for years; others face the prospect of a much-lower expectation for lifestyle, travel and hobbies in those years after work.

How does this dilemma occur, and what can we do to change it?

As we've said, this dilemma occurs because of the myths we believe about trading time for dollars, that it's OK to live for today and pay tomorrow with credit-financing. No worries because we have plenty of time to prepare for tomorrow.

Focusing on current income by working long hours should be a strategy for a relatively short time. The faster one is able to convert labor-produced income into the acquisition of income-producing assets—real estate—the sooner one is no longer dependent on his or her own efforts to produce that income.

It is a myth that has survived generation after generation: a person must work into his or her 60s, or today even the 70s, in order to produce lifestyle income. This is what we have been taught, so we buy in and conform to the models that have been presented by our parents, neighbors and teachers.

Today, Social Security, employment pensions and Medicaid benefits are being reduced due to the government's inability to control its spending. The reliance on third-party assistance can no longer be assured.

Why must one work until a prescribed age before "retirement"? What is retirement anyway? We submit that this is just another myth and lie, a vision of some distant lifestyle where the job or career comes to a close and one can travel, play golf or sit idly without a care in the world.

By building a portfolio of capital assets, one ma y readily become financially free.

Does this make sense? Why should one stop being productive based on an arbitrary age, especially if that productivity is not based directly on the exchange of one's labor for income?

In Chapter 5, we discussed the concept of replacing our labor with the acquisition of capital assets, specifically real estate, that will build our net worth (also known as "future bank") and replace our labor-produced income. By building a portfolio of capital assets, one may readily become financially free and independent of the requirement to work at all, providing what we refer to as Plan B.

CHAPTER KEY TAKEAWAYS

 Most people mistakenly focus on current income, salary or wages as a measure of success.

 Current cash flow meets our current lifestyle needs but does nothing for our future, unless employed in a well-planned investment strategy.

 Our society emphasizes higher education in order to enter a career or profession. For true financial freedom, that career income must be replaced by investment assets.

 The goal should be to convert excess cash flow from the active income side (earned income) to the acquisition of capital assets to produce passive income.

NOTES

_____

_____

_____

_____

_____

_____

_____

_____

_____

PLAN OF ACTION

_____

_____

_____

_____

_____

_____

8 Why Real Estate? Why Now?

PANDEMONIUM BROKE OUT in both the financial and real estate markets when the economy came tumbling down in 2008 and again in the unprecedented shutdown caused by the COVID-19 pandemic. Cycles cause a lot of disruption, which in turn can create chaos. It is within the chaos of the markets that real opportunities occur. It is my premise that we live in such times right now (see Chapter 2, The Great American Wealth Transfer).

Due to the significant economic impact of the COVID shutdown, there will be a large number of assets on sale for investors with capital and access. Foreigners are buying up our real estate as fast as they can, in the belief that the U.S. is still the most stable country in which to invest.

This will be the biggest opportunity to purchase assets on sale since 2008. Opportunities like this only come a few times in a lifetime. I have personally only experienced 3-4 such opportunities in mine. Market resets create large-scale repricing as the recession sorts out the winners from the losers. Those who did not prepare for recession will face cash flow shortages that will force them to sell assets to maintain liquidity. In short, this means that property is available at very large discounts to market value.

While it's possible to purchase capital assets at a discount because of the inefficiency in the real estate market, contrast that with the stock market, bonds, annuity contracts or even gold and precious metals. Every one of those investment assets are bought and sold at full market value on any given day; there are no discounts. One only hopes to buy low and sell later at a higher value.

When buying real estate, there is no centralized marketplace. Sure, one can search for possible good deals by accessing the Multiple Listing Service (MLS), For Sale By Owner (FSBO) on line, and other sites such as Craigslist. This method does work and will produce good leads if a consistent effort is made.

When buying real estate, there is no centralized marketplace.

Many other lead-generation opportunities are available when seeking good deals in today's marketplace. That's what makes real estate such a great and opportunistic investment. No one has the ability to control the whole market—not by any means! Small players can play and profit right along with those who have more money and resources.

Figuratively, we are in the "perfect storm." Values are down, interest rates are historically low, and banks have, for the most part, stopped making loans. Owner-occupants either cannot qualify to purchase homes or are unsure about the economy and their job status and do not want to lock into a purchase that might be difficult to sell later if necessary.

This situation has created a void in the market. Without financing, real estate values decrease. Financing is everything (along with location, of course). Few owner-occupants have the ability to purchase a home without financing options. Without home buyers, the market remains stagnant at best.

Traditionally, real estate might return 6-7% on the actual cash invested on a free and clear house. In today's market conditions, that return may rise to the double-digits. Combine that with the use of leverage and returns well into the double-digits become possible.

Another characteristic of real estate that we have not discussed is the control factor. Real estate is a tangible, or hard, asset as opposed to financial assets, which are "paper assets."

The difference is that if we own a real estate property and that property (or the tenant-occupant) does not perform as desired, a change can be made: a tenant can be evicted and replaced, or the equity can be sold and exchanged for another property in perhaps a better location. (We'll cover property and tenant selection in another chapter.)

Don't worry, if you don't want to ever see a tenant or a toilet, that can be arranged. (It's still important for you to understand the base qualifying criteria for property and tenant selection.)

If one owns stocks (the equity in a company) or bonds (the debt of a company) and neither investment performs as desired, there is little that can be done to change management or systems in order to make those assets perform better. We don't control the management. We either hold on and hope for a better result, or we have to sell at a lower or even distressed valuation and suffer the loss.

What about commercial or multi-family real estate investments? Cash flow and profit can be made in any real estate investment class as long as the investor has knowledge of and uses principled investment strategies to make the investment.

I would advise against these classes for the new investor because commercial and multi-family investments contain many more components that must be analyzed and considered before determining the value or whether the investment is even one that should be made.

Additionally, commercial and multi-family investments generally require a combination of bank or other institutional financing and/or the pooling of money with other investors. (This is known as a syndication; see my Bonus Chapter.) In these scenarios, the individual passive investor has little, if any, control and is dependent on the managing party to create value, manage and produce the cash flow. Also, selling one's interest in such an investment can be difficult should the need for cash liquidity arise.

So what do we recommend to get started? Single-family houses, as the next chapter will discuss, can be thought of as horizontal apartments. Take an apartment building and tip it on its side. The individual apartment units spreading out over the landscape become individual units just like single-family houses.

CHAPTER KEY TAKEAWAYS

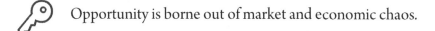 Opportunity is borne out of market and economic chaos.

The lack of a centralized marketplace results in the opportunity for great deals in real estate investment.

We are living in the perfect storm today for real estate investment: interest rates are low, real estate is on sale, and banks are not providing credit to would-be home buyers.

NOTES

_____

_____

_____

_____

_____

_____

_____

_____

_____

PLAN OF ACTION

_____

_____

_____

_____

_____

_____

9 WHY SINGLE-FAMILY HOUSES?

THE POPULATION OF the United States continues to grow and is projected to grow indefinitely. Even though our country's birth rate is lower than it was 50 years ago, our liberal immigration policies allow for a constant influx of new citizens every year. Every person and every family needs a roof over their head.

The most desired rooftop is a single-family house with defined property lines. Homeownership is the American dream. Certainly there are times when apartments make more sense, such as when people are single, more transient or unable to maintain a single-family house.

There will always be a need for both single-family and multi-family homes, but the single-family house is where most people will live throughout most of their lifetime.

Single-family houses provide the "IDEAL":

• **Income** – Properties provide either rental income or interest income (when selling and carrying the financing).

• **Depreciation** – One of the tax benefits of real estate ownership. Additionally, equity or profit gain in a real estate asset may be exchanged into another property or properties through a long-standing IRS regulation known as Chapter 1031 exchanges.

• **Equity** – Equity is created in several ways with real estate: 1) Buying at a discount to market values provides for immediate additional equity in addition to any down payment made; 2) Improvements to the property through renovation and rehabilitation should always add a multiple to equity beyond the actual investment made in improvements; 3) Inflation or "organic appreciation" will increase the value of the asset so that its value maintains par with the purchasing power of its original equity value as inflation devalues other financial assets.

THE BENEFITS OF REAL ESTATE

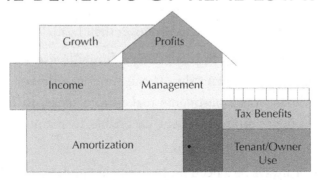

Diagram courtesy of Pete Fortunato

• **Amortization** – The pay-down of debt-financed (leveraged) acquisitions through the cash flow provided by the tenant-occupants will also increase equity.

• **Leverage** – The ability to rapidly grow wealth and equity through capital asset acquisition, if done using specific principles described in this book. See a more-detailed discussion in Chapter 13.

From an investment standpoint, houses, particularly those in conforming subdivision neighborhoods, are relatively easy to evaluate. Property evaluation and due diligence are discussed in Chapter 17. To summarize, a conforming house in a given subdivision in average habitable condition will produce a stable rental income within a relatively small range, 5-10% variance at most.

That same house will also sell in an economic market within a similar sale price range of 5-10%. Variances in property condition will dictate whether a particular property will be high or low within this range. Single-family houses, therefore, are the easiest asset class to evaluate in terms of monthly income and asset value.

The actual condition of a single-family house is relatively easy to determine. Many investors, over time and with experience, are able to perform their own property condition assessment. For those in doubt or for the beginning investor, property inspection services are available at a nominal fee to perform full inspections of both the structural and mechanical components of single-family houses.

These third-party reports not only protect the buyer from unknown defects or deferred maintenance but also allow for a renegotiation of price or terms when such problems are found before the sale transaction closes. Additionally, roofers, plumbers, electricians, foundation experts, etc., can be called in if, after a cursory inspection, an underlying problem is suspected. Many novice investors get themselves into trouble because they forgo inspections before buying a property.

Single-family houses are used by homeowners for shelter, not as an investment. Many traditional financial planners include a person's home as an asset on the financial statement. We don't believe a home is an asset in the same way that other investment assets are. A home is really a necessary liability. A home requires maintenance, repairs and replacements.

A homeowner places a value on his or her home not for the income potential, as an investor would, but because a particular home in a particular city and neighborhood fits the needs of his or her family.

The purchase price of the home will be a definite consideration, but it is the monthly payment relative to the purchase price and current bank interest rates that affects the value of houses. In short, the value of single-family houses is tied more to general economic markets than to the capitalization rates used by investors to evaluate multi-family and commercial properties.

When a house is put on the market for sale, as long as that house has been satisfactorily maintained and is located in a market desirable to families, the value of that house will be determined by the market value placed by potential owner-occupants—not investors.

Because the U.S. government and our society at large place a great deal of importance and social status on the American dream of homeownership, single-family houses will always be an asset class somewhat protected and even subsidized by our federal government.

Bank and mortgage loans are subsidized by the Federal National Mortgage Association, aka Fannie Mae; the Federal Home Loan Mortgage Corporation, aka Freddie Mac; the Federal Housing Administration (FHA); and the Veterans Administration (VA), all funded by taxpayer money. These federal giants serve to provide very affordable fixed rate and long-term financing for single-family housing.

Additionally, the government subsidizes the cost of homeownership by providing for a specific tax deduction to homeowners, who may then reduce taxable and reportable income by the amount of interest paid on a home mortgage, thus reducing the amount of taxes paid each year.

You may or may not agree with federal subsidies for homeownership. The fact is, it is there and is likely to continue because the voting populace values its ability to afford and purchase a home. As an investor, you are able to tap into this subsidy as a benefactor of these programs simply because you invest in single-family homes.

Few other investments enjoy this same benefit on a continual basis. This provides a great deal of stability to the single-family house investment—a factor that every investor desires.

What About Multi-Family and Commercial Real Estate?

Our bias toward single-family houses as capital investments is outlined in this chapter. Other asset classes, such as commercial, multi-family and mobile home parks, offer lucrative investment opportunities for those who are able to make a specialty niche in these areas. But for the rank-and-file investor who simply wants a relatively safe and fast track to financial freedom and security, single-family house investments are a great place to start.

The analysis and due diligence required prior to purchasing the other real estate asset classes are much more detailed and sophisticated. For example, EPA (Environmental Protection Agency) testing of such sites will run several thousand dollars. Surveys, along with other mechanical and structural inspections, also involve more time and expense. Local-government code and zoning issues must be understood and worked through.

Funding of larger asset classes generally requires bank institutional funding and/or pooling of investor funds into partnership or LLC entities with a general manager involved.

For the small investor, being a part of a fund or entity investment group is the most likely point of entrance to commercial or multi-family investing. It comes, however, with a loss of control, as there has to be a great reliance on the managing partner.

This person is usually in charge of locating, negotiating, closing and managing the project until it is eventually sold. If this person or company does a good job and is proficient in its management, the investors remain passive and receive a desired return.

Too often, even the best intentions go awry.

Too often, even the best intentions go awry. Large syndicators and fund managers are often under a great deal of pressure to perform, which means that acquisitions are made that are not particularly good and the management during the holding period may be sub par.

Most syndicators and fund managers take a sizable commission or fee on the front end of these projects—that is how they make their living. Once they get their fee, they are often on to the next deal, and the management of the current deal is not high on their priority list.

Again, if an investor wishes to invest in larger-asset classes in this way, my advice is to be sure to do a lot of due diligence on the principals in the management company. (For more on investing in syndications, see the Bonus Chapter.) Realize, too, that the people you might be dealing with today, those making you the promises of cash flow returns and equity profit gains, may be gone tomorrow.

CHAPTER KEY TAKEAWAYS

🔑 Investments in houses provide stability and control when acquired properly.

🔑 Single family houses provide the following benefits: use, income, depreciation, equity, amortization and leverage.

🔑 Houses are relatively easy to evaluate. Third-party licensed inspectors may be utilized to confirm property condition before the investment is made.

🔑 Houses provide geographic and demographic diversity.

🔑 Houses will always be a "protected" and somewhat subsidized asset in this country.

NOTES

_____

_____

_____

_____

_____

_____

_____

_____

_____

PLAN OF ACTION

_____

_____

_____

_____

_____

_____

10 EQUITY AND DEBT INVESTMENTS

THE SCOPE OF this book is limited to single-family real estate investments for the reasons outlined in Chapter 9. Other real estate asset classes, such as multi-family and commercial, would require a depth of analysis not possible here.

Single-family investments afford a great deal of flexibility and safety. Many investors specialize in single-family residential for those reasons and do not stray into other asset categories. Diversifying and becoming educated and astute in other real estate asset classes is a personal decision and should be considered once the basics of financing, leverage and management are understood within the single-family residential class.

The due diligence for a single-family house investment is not difficult and can be easily handled by novice investors. The two basic single-family investments are equity (or property ownership) and debt (or lender-secured investments). The latter is the preferred investment for the passive investor, although equity investments can be structured to have one active and one passive co-venture partner.

1. **Equity investments** – An equity investment implies direct ownership. In this investment example, you will hold title to the single-family residence property, either in your name or in an entity such as an LLC. As the owner with title, you hold the "superior" position—you have the ultimate control over the property. Your catalyst co-venture partner usually will hold a management contract and option to document his or her interests in the property.

The management contract allows your co-venture partner to manage the property (as the passive investor, you don't want to deal with management and tenants) and defines the split or sharing of the net cash flow. Your co-venture partner also needs to document his/her future equity position in the property by using an option.

An option is simply a future right to purchase an interest in a property for a specific price and terms. In this way, the active or catalyst investor must satisfactorily manage the equity investment (the property) to earn the right to purchase a 50% (or other) interest in the property.

2. **Debt investments** – A debt investment is similar to being "the bank." Most people who buy a home have not saved the total purchase price in cash and therefore need a loan from a bank to complete the purchase. Banks make their money and profit by lending cash to worthy individuals and businesses, charging an interest rate for the use of the money, and securing the loan or "promise to pay" to the specific asset being purchased, such as a home, new car or business equipment.

Private lenders who wish to invest in real estate without the hassles, responsibility and liability of ownership find that being a debt-lender like a bank is a viable method of investing in good real estate. The process and the documentation are no different than what a bank uses to make loans.

Shared Appreciation Loans

Lenders are always concerned about inflation and the loss of purchasing power of the income received on the loan over many years. Here are three ways lenders offset the inflationary devaluation of money:

1. **Short-term loans** – Many loans are written on the basis of a longer pay-back period (amortization schedule), such as 20, 25 or 30 years. For a fixed-rate loan, one in which the interest rate does not change during the term of the loan, 20 or 30 years would be a very long commitment without some way to offset future inflation.

Some lenders have short-term "call" or "balloon" provisions written into the loan agreement, which means that at the three- or five-year period, the bank can "call" the loan due. That enables the bank to renew the loan at current interest rates, allowing for higher returns if inflation has lowered the value of the currency being used to pay back the loan.

2. **Variable-rate loans** – Another method is to allow for interest rate adjustments during the term of the loan. The ability for the lender to adjust the interest rate is usually tied to a common interest rate index that mirrors the effects of inflation.

3. **Shared appreciation** – A third method of offsetting inflation for the lender is to use language in the promissory note that allows for sharing or participation in the equity of the collateral property when the loan term has completed, or when the loan is refinanced or paid off when the property is sold.

In this case, the lender receives the return of the original loan, all accrued interest and a stated percentage of the net equity (profit) over a certain amount.

Shared appreciation is generally safer for the borrower, as the monthly payment and interest rate do not adjust. In this case, the borrower trades money today against future wealth-building.

Bear in mind that making loans to consumers or owner-occupants has become more difficult in recent years. The Dodd-Frank Consumer Protection Act of 2010 has added an immense amount of new regulation to consumer-lending practices. Extending credit (financing) to owner occupants who will use a house as their primary residence requires a high level of compliance and licensing today.

It is the author's recommendation that investors not make a practice of lending to owner-occupants and restrict their investment lending to non-owner occupants (businesses or investors).

CHAPTER KEY TAKEAWAYS

 Equity investments imply ownership and require direct management of the asset.

 Debt investments are similar to being "the bank" and provide a more passive investment return.

 Shared or equity appreciation loans can provide cash flow, capital gain profits and an inflation hedge.

 Loans or extension of credit to home owner occupants is regulated today by the Dodd-Frank Consumer Protection Act and requires additional steps and cautions for the investor extending such credit.

NOTES

_____

_____

_____

_____

_____

_____

_____

_____

_____

PLAN OF ACTION

_____

_____

_____

_____

_____

_____

11 INFLATION — THE HIDDEN TAX

HISTORICALLY, COUNTRIES WITH poor financial controls—spending more money than the revenue they take in and covering the shortfall with ever-increasing debt—find that the least politically damaging cure is through the devaluation of their currency. When it takes more of a given currency to pay for the same services or products (seen by the citizens as rising prices and wages), inflation is in play.

Inflation always serves the debtor by allowing him or her to repay the debt with cheaper currency. In essence, inflation is a hidden tax that a country's government assesses on its citizens without any government collection efforts.

Think about buying a basket of consumable items at a local WalMart. If $350 would fill one large grocery cart with goods today, how many carts could the $350 have filled five years ago? A cart and a half. What about 10, 15, 20 or 30 years ago?

Inflation decreases the purchasing power of our dollars so that, as time goes on, we need more dollars to pay for the same housing, utilities, groceries, pharmaceuticals and cars. Being on a "fixed income" in an inflationary environment will quickly decrease the lifestyle of those whose retirement cash flow does not have an inflation hedge built in.

Inflation is the friend of those who understand debt-leveraging and are able to use it in their investment protocol. By utilizing the safe leveraging techniques outlined in this book, the debtor is able to control more of his/her tangible or real assets that will retain value in a hyper-inflationary market, and the debt being repaid will be paid with dollars that are worth less and less as time goes on. This is, in effect, a strategy to short the dollar.

Inflation is the enemy of those who take the conservative approach to investment planning. In short, those who are prudent and save, minimizing credit and becoming debt-free (the formula given by many well-known financial gurus), will be penalized in an inflationary environment. It doesn't seem to make sense and certainly is not fair. Unfortunately, we must deal with the reality of "what is" and not what we hoped would be or what we believe is the most conservative and risk-averse in our financial planning.

What about lenders? The asset value of a lender (a bank or private lender) is reduced by inflation as long as the income stream from the promissory note is fixed by a monthly payment and interest rate. As mentioned above: with inflation, dollars received next year, in five years or in 10 years will be worth far less in purchasing power than they are today.

More about lending and income streams secured by real estate will be discussed in a future chapter. At this point, let's simply state the fact that there are ways to index those payment or income streams so that inflation does not devalue the purchasing power of the dollars received.

This is an important concept to grasp, since this book is written on the premise that good returns secured by real estate can be done on a passive basis without the loss of buying power through the inflationary process.

CHAPTER KEY TAKEAWAYS

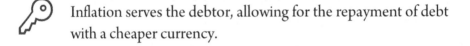

Inflation serves the debtor, allowing for the repayment of debt with a cheaper currency.

Inflation is the enemy of those who are conservative, hold cash or equivalent assets, and invest in bank CDs or savings accounts.

Those who acquire good capital assets (real estate) with prudent leverage can profit very handsomely in inflationary markets.

Lenders who hold paper or loans that are fixed for many years may find their investment value declining with the onset of more inflation.

NOTES

_____

_____

_____

_____

_____

_____

_____

_____

_____

PLAN OF ACTION

_____

_____

_____

_____

_____

_____

12 TAXES – THE NO. 1 ENEMY OF WEALTH BUILDING

FEDERAL, STATE AND local taxes are already on the rise. Past exemptions and deductions are being stripped away. The government has a very strong appetite for money, and taxation has always been the primary method of feeding that appetite.

To make matters worse, those in the top 10% of wealth in this country pay 70% of the taxes; 50% of the population pays no taxes at all. Fewer are doing the work to carry the load of those receiving entitlement benefits.

This is a course that is not sustainable, but until there is a financial catastrophe, those who produce will be expected and required to pay more to subsidize those who cannot pay or refuse to be responsible for their own consumption.

Those in the top 10% of wealth in this country pay 70% of the taxes.

Here's an example of how detrimental taxation can be to the capitalist entrepreneur and wealth-builder:

If one dollar is doubled every year for 20 years, in year two there are two dollars, in year three there are four dollars, in year four there are eight dollars, 16, 32, 64 and so on. At year 20 the doubling factor will have grown the original one dollar to $1 million.

Amazing, yes? Except that we did not factor in for taxes. At a 15% tax bracket—that is, removing 15% of the earnings each year before doubling again—that same dollar after 20 years only grows to $250,000. At a 28% tax rate, the growth is reduced to $51,000. And at 39%, the top marginal rate, that same dollar doubled over 20 years will grow only to a paltry $13,000.

The taxes we pay play a significant role in our ability to grow our wealth and create financial freedom! By structuring the way we receive income and how we set up our business models, it is possible to greatly reduce the effect of taxation.

None of us likes to pay taxes, yet we know they are inevitable. Most of us have financial advisers who assist in the reporting of income and expenses, but that is usually done historically, after the fact. Few take the time to plan and be proactive in order to minimize the effect of taxes. If they did, real estate would stand out as the best investment asset to use in increasing wealth with the lowest possible tax.

Considering the example just given, reducing the tax rate on investment capital by even 13% can mean a difference in growth by a factor of 5! It follows, then, that by using tax-reduction strategies, a person may be able to reduce the amount of time required to build wealth by the same factor of 5.

Don't underestimate the power of utilizing the tax strategies available through real estate investments and the use of self-directed retirement accounts such as an IRA or a 401(k). The specific strategies will be covered in more detail in future chapters.

CHAPTER KEY TAKEAWAYS

 Conservative savers are penalized by artificially low interest rates.

 Those in the top 10% of wealth pay 70% of the taxes... and it's only going to get worse.

 Real estate investment provides a number of tax-advantaged opportunities not available with other investment classes.

Real estate investments may be made through self-directed qualified retirement plans such as 401(k)s, IRAs, Health Savings Accounts and Coverdell Education Savings Accounts.

NOTES

_____

_____

_____

_____

_____

_____

_____

_____

_____

PLAN OF ACTION

_____

_____

_____

_____

_____

_____

13   LEVERAGE - THE DOUBLE-EDGED SWORD

LEVERAGE IS A term not readily understood by many. Leverage is neither good nor bad; it all depends on how leverage is used and under what circumstances. In common terms, leverage is simply getting more from less, whether through one's own labor, by mechanical advantage or by utilizing other resources (both human and/or other assets).

Leverage is often used in combination with financial formulas, as in "financial leverage." The use of borrowed money, or debt, in order to control, own or use an asset without having to pay for the asset in full, or without having to save the capital necessary to pay for the asset in full, is a form of financial leverage.

The use of leverage in financial wealth-building is key to reaching goals or achieving financial freedom much more quickly than an "earn and save" formula. There are many who endorse the use of institutional or bank mortgage debt to acquire investment properties. It makes sense in theory, due to the low interest rates of the past two decades. However, bank loans are recourse loans, meaning that you, the borrower, are subjecting all of your personal assets to guarantee the loan.

There is a great deal of fine print in commercial loans that can cause financial issues to the borrower. In other words, the bank institution holds all of the cards. If you are going to go this route, understand the risks. This type of leverage is what caused many real estate investors to lose hundreds of thousands of dollars of equity when the housing market collapsed in 2008.

Safe forms of financial leverage include terms of sale from the seller of the property (also known as owner-financing or seller-financing). In this case, it is generally easy to negotiate terms with the seller that are much more favorable than bank institutional loans, which often have three- or five-year balloon or call positions and require full personal recourse along with applications, financial statements and rigorous underwriting.

> *The use of bank-loan financing for the acquisition of investments is not recommended.*

Many who lost equity were not true investors; they were in the business of real estate, attempting to "flip" houses for short-term profits. That business model contains a relative degree of risk and is not covered in this book.

Banks are tightly regulated by the federal government, allowing little room for re-negotiation or leniency if an investor falls into a difficult time. Additionally, many of the investors who failed were highly leveraged (100% or more) with relatively short-term loans.

Investors who avoided bank financing and used one of the other forms of financial leverage discussed in this book were able to weather the economic downturn without significant loss. In fact, investors who maintained a disciplined and strategic approach to real estate investment (buy-and-hold vs. flipping and speculation) were able to buy at steep discounts with high rates of return on cash invested.

Personally, I have used bank financing only five (5) times in forty years and hundreds of direct ownership real estate investments. One of my early real estate mentors, Jack Miller, said "Only those who are lazy and lack creativity become beholden to the banks." I will continue to thank Jack for the rest of my life for embedding those words into my soul.

The strategic investor is able to ride the normal economic cycles and make significant equity gains, while those with no plan often suffer the consequences of a lack of principled investing models.

Sources of Non-Bank Financing

Private lenders, the focus of this book, are a great source of investment funds, and they come without the risk that institutional loans create. Dealing with real people rather than institutions provides the safety that allows real estate investors to leverage, create equity and receive cash flow that benefits them a factor of several times over paying all cash.

Sellers who, through negotiation, can be enticed to carry some or the majority of their equity in financing for the buyer (seller- or owner-financing) is another form of financial leverage that many investors completely miss.

Besides being a method of selling property more quickly than for all-cash (which many times means a buyer must obtain new bank financing, a very time-consuming and arduous task today), the seller may find tax advantages to carrying the financing, as well as an interest yield return higher than what is offered by bank savings, CDs or money market accounts.

A third form of non-bank financial leverage is the purchase of property "subject to" an existing loan, that is, a loan that is currently secured by the subject property. This may be a bank or mortgage loan or a private lender loan.

By taking title subject to the existing loan, the buyer acknowledges that the loan exists and must be paid, although the buyer does not assume personal liability for the obligation to pay that loan. In layman's terms, yes, this loan must be paid or the lender could foreclose, but as long as the new buyer simply makes the payments, the buyer benefits by the use of this already existing financing.

One small caveat to buying subject to an existing loan: All bank or institutional financing documents and the majority of private financing documents will contain in the security agreement (mortgage or deed of trust) what is known as the "due on sale" clause.

This clause provides that in the event the buyer who executed the documents for the loan sells or otherwise transfers title of the property to another owner, the lender has the right to "call" the loan immediately due.

In other words, the "due on sale" clause provides that a lender—who originally provided loan terms of perhaps 15, 20, or 30 years—does not have to allow those loan terms to be transferred to subsequent buyers. Since most houses are sold on average every five to seven years, this provides the lender with a reasonable expectation to receive the principal balance of the loan back in that period of time so that it may be re-lent at then-current interest rates.

In the era of low interest rates, the majority of institutional banks and mortgage lenders are not enforcing the "due on sale" clause... as long as the payments continue to be made on a timely basis and the property taxes and insurance (normally held in an escrow account by the lender) are paid.

We do not think this leniency toward the "due on sale" clause will continue indefinitely. At some point the housing market will find stability, the inventory of defaulted loans and foreclosed houses will have cycled through the market, and banks will take a more aggressive stance regarding the "due on sale" clause.

Taking title subject to an existing loan is, at best, a short-term financing strategy for acquisition of property and should not be relied on for long-term hold strategies.

Estate-builders can use the power of leverage to enhance their ability to increase their wealth and equity much faster than if they earn, save, invest and then pay all cash for a property.

This could be a younger person building his or her career and family base, or a middle-aged or older person who has suffered financial losses from poor or speculative investments or simply has not had the discipline to make regular investing part of a good financial habit.

The proper use of leverage is key to building financial wealth and freedom.

CHAPTER KEY TAKEAWAYS

 Leverage is neither good nor bad; it depends on how it is used.

 The proper use of leverage is a key to wealth-building and reaching financial freedom.

The use of private lending in the acquisition of real estate investments is far superior and safer than using bank or institutional debt financing.

Estate-builders use the power of leverage to reach financial goals much faster than those who earn, save and pay all cash for real estate investments.

NOTES

_____

_____

_____

_____

_____

_____

_____

_____

_____

_____

PLAN OF ACTION

_____

_____

_____

_____

_____

_____

14 JOINT VENTURES – THE KEY TO YOUR INVESTMENT SUCCESS

WE HAVE NOTED in previous chapters the benefits of joint venture investing in real estate assets. This chapter will go deeper, breaking down exactly how this works and how the separate or severable interests are created.

Too often, because we are taught at an early age the importance of being self-reliant, we tend to go it alone in life and work, believing that collaboration and seeking cooperative relationships are signs of weakness. Quite the opposite is true—those who understand the value of associates and partners are able to combine efforts and complementary skills to create much more than can be created by just one.

Let's look next at the anatomy of a real estate transaction investment or "deal." There are four essential parts to every deal:

1. **Sourcing the deal** – Knowing where and how to find "good deals" is both an art and a science. It involves lead-generation marketing combined with market knowledge and an active network with

other principal players, such as bankers, CPAs, attorneys, real estate brokers, title company representatives, insurance agents and other investors.

Those who can produce good leads on deals (often called property locators, bird dogs or wholesalers) can make an active living by doing so.

2. **Structuring, negotiating and closing the deal** – Good deals aren't found; opportunities are found, and the good deals are created by the knowledge, ability and negotiating skills of the active partner. The active partner may have his or her own lead-generating systems and network and/or may rely on others who source good lead opportunities.

Turning the opportunity into a closed good deal takes time, patience and experience. This is not a job for the novice investor, who would be better served by investing capital with an active partner who can fulfill this part of the investment transaction.

3. **Capital to fund the deal** – This is where the passive co-venture partner most often participates. Cash may be necessary to fund a discounted opportunity (when no seller-financing or taking title subject to the loan makes sense or cannot be negotiated).

Or, there may be only a portion of the acquisition cost for which private capital is needed, and the remaining financial leverage is carried by the seller or taken subject to an existing loan. A third reason for private capital would be for rehab and renovation of the property.

If the private lender is needed for only a portion of the investment funding, then the return on that investment should be in some way proportionate to the percentage of funding provided.

4. **Managing the deal to exit** – Managing the deal to the agreed-upon exit point is a key to the cash flow and equity gain in any deal.

Good managers can make a good living managing other people's assets for a fee and, for those who are wise, also for an equity position. (This goes back to the premise of transitioning from trading time for dollars to freedom through capital asset acquisition.)

Management of a joint venture deal will include any front-end property renovation or repairs, as well as tenant management and continued maintenance until the property is one day sold or exchanged by mutual agreement of the parties.

Each of the four primary parts of every investment is individually important. No one part can reach the desired outcome without the others. Some people mistakenly believe that "their money" is the most important part of the equation. They believe that without their money, the deal can't be done.

While the capital to fund the acquisition is important, today there is more money chasing "good investment deals." Trillions of dollars are sitting on the sidelines, inactive, in savings, CDs, money markets and other low- or non-interest-bearing accounts simply due to fear or a lack of a connection to or understanding of real estate markets.

> *One does not have to be 100% active or 100% passive in any particular deal.*

Money is money, and no one person has a lock on available cash looking for a good investment home.

One does not have to be 100% active or 100% passive in any particular deal. Many deals may involve an experienced partner who mentors a less experienced but willing active partner in how to find, negotiate, close and manage these deals.

In this example, the passive partner may be considered "semi-active," as he or she will provide time to educate and coach the novice partner, who will be responsible for the active management.

In such a case, the splits of the joint venture deal may be more fa-vorable to the semi-active, experienced partner until which time the novice partner becomes more capable of handling the investment from beginning to end and only needs capital to fund some of the deals.

The point is, there is no "one way" to structure a joint venture. Each one is constructed based on the parties involved and the spe-cifics of the deal.

This chapter is meant to be more of a reference guide and starting point for people who will continue to build on the joint venture con-cept. There are any number of applicable deviations from what's described here that will work well in an individual's own investment arena.

CHAPTER KEY TAKEAWAYS

 Structuring investments with other people who compliment you is the fast track to wealth-building.

 One can be active or passive in any investment deal.

 There are four main components to every real estate investment transaction:

1. Sourcing the deal

2. Structuring, negotiating and closing the deal

3. Securing capital to fund the deal

4. Managing the deal to the exit (sale or refinance)

NOTES

_____

_____

_____

_____

_____

_____

_____

_____

PLAN OF ACTION

_____

_____

_____

_____

_____

15 Managing Your Real Estate Investments – Or Not

THE BIGGEST PROBLEM that novice real estate investors face is management. Traditional real-estate investment models involve wannabe investors taking a few weekend classes or purchasing books, then jumping into the water as a "real estate investor" with visions of riches and income beyond their wildest dreams.

A property is found, a contract is executed, and within a few weeks the new investor is a "property owner," aka a "landlord."

A fundamental problem with most of these "get rich quick" seminars, books or home-study courses is that they leave out the glamorous job of tenant management. Somehow, all of that rental income will be automatic once the house is purchased.

One or two houses into the game plan and the new investor is stressed. He/she is an accidental landlord! The property investment perhaps was acquired as a result of said weekend seminar or home study course, or because a house wouldn't sell or maybe was an inheritance.

In any case, an accidental landlord has no management skills. This responsibility is usually given minimal lip service and left out of the equation.

Do not fear. In this book, we neither omit nor sugarcoat any aspect of real estate investment. Management does exist, and it must be handled as a business, not a hobby. Systems, protocol and documentation must be set up in advance, even for the first property. Without this infrastructure, it becomes management-by-trial until the new investor becomes a motivated seller. This is not the desired plan.

> *Do not fear. In this book, we neither omit nor sugarcoat any aspect of real estate investment.*

Returning full circle to the premise of this book, a person can be a catalyst, an active real estate investor or a passive investor, creating joint ventures with those who are active players in the market.

For the passive investor, management is handled by the active or managing joint venture partner. As outlined in Chapter 10, this can be done either with equity (owner or title-holding) investments or with debt (lender-position investments).

Either way, the passive investor is not put into the position of active manager. Voila! Problem solved.

The passive investor is responsible for performing proper due diligence on the person proposed as the active managing co-venture partner, and at least overseeing and verifying the due diligence and evaluation on the property provided by the managing partner.

One cannot be blind to being educated enough to make these basic evaluations. If problems are to occur with the joint venture structure, this is where the breakdown usually occurs.

Finally, before the deal is closed both joint venture partners have a duty and obligation to agree on the mutual expectations of the specific deal. Who is going to be responsible for what? (This will be documented with the paperwork; see Chapter 20.)

What are the mutual expectations regarding the anticipated holding period of the property? If the property is positioned in a marketplace where a quick renovation and resale to another investor or owner-occupant is the goal, then that should be specified in the discussions.

Always have a Plan B—if the property does not sell for the desired price within a certain period of time, the two partners should have a defined directive to move the property to a longer-term hold and rent it out until market conditions improve and the property can be placed back on the market.

There is nothing wrong with an active or passive partner being involved together or with other partners in short-term retail "flips" or "quick-turns" and in longer-term buy-and-holds.

There is no right or wrong, although each party should have a definite purpose behind every deal that is done. This should be part of an overall "Freedom Blueprint" that will take that person to the freedom point as quickly as possible.

What if one partner needs out of the joint venture early?

Even with mutual expectations well laid out, events and circumstances in life can change a partner's needs and immediate goals. Particularly with longer-term buy-and-hold investments, one party may find himself or herself in a position where a cash infusion would solve a problem. (We define long term to be at least five years, although 10 years is a better length for a good deal to mature.)

How is this handled in a joint venture agreement? Recall that the joint venture agreements as described in this book allow for the separate or "severable" interests of each party. Unless the contract is written as non-transferable or non-assignable, each party's interest in the investment deal, both cash flow and equity, can be transferred to a third party.

There may be a good reason to make the managing partner's management responsibility and interest non-transferable or non-assignable, if for no other reason than the passive-lender partner relied on the character and experience of the managing partner when the original deal structure was made.

On the other hand, the passive party, usually the lender, has an interest in the property that is not usually dependent on any skill or expertise once the deal is closed and being managed. There would be less at stake for the managing partner if the passive partner's interest was assigned to another party.

The ability to assign or transfer severable interests is a negotiable item. Again, whether such assignment is allowed at one party's sole discretion or whether it requires mutual consent should be negotiated and set up one way or the other on purpose.

When in doubt, we recommend making the assignability of severable interests not allowed. Then, if a situation occurred where one party needed out of the joint venture, the assignability could be negotiated so that the remaining partner could approve the new partner.

For example, if the passive-lender partner's interest was held in a debt-financed joint venture with a promissory note and security agreement to document the use of some or all of his/her capital to fund the deal, that promissory note and security agreement could be assigned to another investor who would pay "market value for that interest."

Here's a common objection to the joint venture model: "If I joint-venture with someone else, then my overall return on investment will be less than if I did it all and controlled it all myself." That's what we call a scarcity mindset. If that is your mindset, let's see if we can change it.

We work off of what is called an abundance mindset. There are more good deals and more opportunities available than any one person can find, negotiate and acquire.

By leveraging joint venture relationships, more deals are done, with each person able to devote his or her time to what he or she does best. This is the most efficient way to build one's wealth and future passive-income streams. Participating in more deals provides diversification as well.

Think about it this way: Where is your time best used? What is the value of your time? If your time is best utilized working in your job, career or profession, then that is how you should spend your working hours, not learning to manage rental property.

By sharing the overall returns with your active co-venture partner, your return will be "good enough" and you will not have the stress or extra work required to manage this new investment. Spend your discretionary time on hobbies and leisure activities with your family. After all, that's what freedom is all about.

Your active co-venture managing partner will handle the management details. That person already has a proven track record (partner due diligence is discussed in Chapter 16). This is the business of the active partner, who spends his or her working hours finding, negotiating, closing and then managing these investment properties for a share of the cash flow and equity.

This is what the active partner does. Let him/her do it.

What about control? With a single-family investment, there usually is no need for multiple investors (pooling of investor money), which might also involve security regulations and licensing (a topic beyond this book). With one active co-venture partner and one passive partner, the benefits of the investment deal (who gets what) are easily documented in writing into "severable interests."

Severable interests indicate investor positions that are negotiable and can be liquidated or transferred without consensus of the other partners. This is the primary difference between a joint venture and a partnership.

Partnerships generally involve two or more parties that together have a percentage interest in the whole of the investment or business opportunity. Premature division of the percentage interests is difficult and will almost always involve legal negotiations and, sometimes, legal battles.

If a managing co-venture partner does not perform, the security documents that define the severable (separate) interests of each party allow for one party to strip the interests from the non-performing partner or, at a minimum, renegotiate the returns to each party. This is not as complicated as it might sound.

Before commencing with any investment structure that involves other investors, you should review your plan with a CPA and an attorney who have experience in these areas.

CHAPTER KEY TAKEAWAYS

Management companies rarely produce satisfactory results for investors—consider utilizing joint ventures instead.

Management of the real estate investment is often omitted from "get rich quick" programs.

Understanding how to manage property effectively can be the difference between profit and loss.

Due diligence of the management company or managing partner should never be overlooked.

NOTES

_____

_____

_____

_____

_____

_____

_____

_____

_____

PLAN OF ACTION

_____

_____

_____

_____

_____

_____

16 Due Dilligence Of The Joint Venture Partner

WHO IS THIS co-venture partner and where do I find him or her?

This is where what we call "relationship capital" becomes one of your most important resources. Your network is your net worth. The people you know—not just superficially, but on a level where you genuinely understand their goals, desires and visions—are your greatest allies in reaching your goals. As Zig Ziglar famously said: "You can have everything in life that you want if you just help enough other people get what they want."

You've put in the effort to build your network and relationships through BNI (a business networking group), Meet-up groups, the National Real Estate Investor Association (REIA) or local Chamber of Commerce meetings and socials.

At least three or four people you have met are involved in some aspect of real estate investment, including single-family investments, which is where you have decided to start. How do you know if an investor knows his/her stuff and can produce solid results?

After a discussion with a potential catalyst investor about the types of deals he or she generally does, it's time to document deals that have been done. When negotiating with the Soviets, Ronald Reagan said: "Trust, but verify." This is the time to verify.

This is not a time to become bashful or apologetic because your level of knowledge and experience is not up to par with your co-venture partner candidate. Any investor worth his or her salt will have no problem providing detail and documentation of a track record.

This should include contracts used to purchase property and HUD-1 closing statements (funding documents used by title companies or attorneys to show the purchase price, down payment, funding, closing costs and tax proration of a real estate transaction).

There is a HUD-1 or settlement document for every property when it is purchased and when it is sold. If a property is being held as a rental investment, there should be a lease or rental agreement providing the terms of occupancy for each tenant who has occupied the property since the date of acquisition. Within a property file should also be receipts for work or maintenance done during the holding period.

It would be wise to do a drive-by of several properties your potential joint venture partner has under his/her current management control. Also, drive by several properties he/she has purchased, fixed and flipped (sold retail to an owner-occupant). This will give you a good idea of the quality of the properties and the neighborhood demographics of his/her investment areas.

You should be comfortable with what you see: Are the houses and neighborhood generally well-kept? Is the area a place where people and families would want to live? Are good schools, churches and shopping nearby, and is there access to jobs?

These are the properties and neighborhoods that will hold their value and attract better and more stable tenants. If you are uncomfortable with what you see, you need to investigate deeper before moving forward with this investor.

Finally, ask for references. Your investor will need to give authorization, either verbal or written and in advance, to people you can call for the information and verifications you want. People asked to be references should include such professionals as a banker, a CPA and an attorney.

You do not want to begin your real estate investment with a novice investor.

It also would be good to call investors your potential investor has worked with. We suggest you speak with three or four past investors, plus several current ones. You do not want to begin your real estate investment with a novice investor.

A track record and references are everything at this point, until you become more experienced yourself in evaluating potential good deals and, if desired, orchestrating any renovations.

What title company does the potential investor normally work with? Ask the closing agent how organized your investor is before and during closing. Are there issues that often surface between the buyer and seller? Are documents provided on time, and does funding occur smoothly?

Check the insurance history of your potential investor. Call his/her agent and ask if there have been any claims in the past five years and under what circumstances. Are insurance policies always paid on time?

Property taxes are usually easy to check. Most counties or taxing jurisdictions in the U.S. are on line, and properties and tax payments can be checked there. Look at a handful of the properties your investor has provided you as reference properties and see whether taxes were paid when due.

Finally, find out what others in the local investing community have to say about this person. Local real estate markets are very close-knit and one's reputation is quickly established, be it positive or negative.

How is this investor perceived by his or her peer group of investors? Is he or she well-respected and greeted warmly, or does there appear to be an aura of distance and polite acknowledgment?

If your investigation produces something you are not sure about, that doesn't necessarily mean you don't want to do business with this person. But it is a sign that you need to dig deeper to be sure you understand specific circumstances.

Most important, you want a potential co-venture partner who is open and honest. Any investor with real experience will have some "war stories" to tell. These stories or incidents should be volunteered—you shouldn't have to dig for everything.

You want to know what this person has dealt with and, when faced with problems, how they were handled. We like a veteran investor who has some scars but also a track record of doing what is right, fulfilling his/her promises and being candid with the people with whom he/she works.

A co-venture partner can be your best friend and ally, or your worst nightmare. This is another relationship in your life, a business relationship. Treat it as such—be thorough, don't disregard your instincts—and your investment activities will be fruitful.

CHAPTER KEY TAKEAWAYS

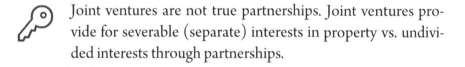

Joint ventures are not true partnerships. Joint ventures provide for severable (separate) interests in property vs. undivided interests through partnerships.

Your network is your net worth. Never underestimate the power of those who can help you and those you can help.

The character of those with whom you might joint venture is every bit as important as the quality of the investment deal.

Co-venturing with others in investment transactions is a form of leverage.

NOTES

_____

_____

_____

_____

_____

_____

_____

_____

_____

PLAN OF ACTION

_____

_____

_____

_____

_____

_____

17 Due Dilligence Of The Property

NOW THAT WE have a good understanding of why real estate makes sense and how we can make investments in real estate without spending lots of time dealing with tenants or toilets, we have to determine the criteria that should be considered in evaluating whether the proposed investment is a good deal or not.

For our example, we will assume that the subject investment property will be held as a rental* at least one year (qualifying the property for long-term capital-gains tax treatment vs. higher ordinary income tax rates).

The business of real estate can also involve buying a single-family property, fixing or rehabbing it, and selling it into the retail marketplace, usually to an owner-occupant. Some, however, are sold to investors as turn-key rental properties.

The chief criteria for evaluating a property are size, location, floor plan, updates, gross scheduled rent, price and/or terms, and investment-to-value ratio.

1. **Size** – Ideal is three bedrooms and two baths with 1,200 square feet or more of living area heated and cooled. A two-car attached garage is desired, although if the neighborhood standard is a single-car garage or carport, that would be considered conforming.

The point is, you want your single-family property investments to be "cookie-cutter" for the neighborhood you choose as your target area. You do not want to be investing in a non-traditional or non-conforming property.

Remember, it's not whether you like the house or think it makes sense. It is about the tenant or owner-occupant. The more conforming your property is to the local area, the wider its appeal for stable rental income and, when the time is right, its sale.

2. **Location** – The property should be located in a standard subdivision in an area that is stable, near good schools, shopping and churches, and accessible to jobs. Other similar houses should surround the subject property 360 degrees.

Having a rental house adjacent to an apartment complex or commercial or industrial zones will diminish its value. Busy side streets or thoroughfares are generally not a benefit unless the acquisition is for future commercial development.

3. **Floor plan** – The floor plan should be normal and conform to the local area.

4. **Updates** – Properties with fixtures, floor coverings, paint and appliances updated within a few years will produce a higher income and better applicants.

5. **Gross scheduled rent** – Determining a conservative monthly rent for a property should be easy, assuming it is in the location described (a standard subdivision where all of the houses are fairly similar in size and with a similar number of bedrooms and baths).

6. **Price and/or terms** – If the subject property is being paid for in cash, it is easy to determine the maximum offer that the investor can make to produce a desired return on investment. For example, if the investor requires an 8% cash-on-cash return on investment, he/she can begin with gross rents and back into the maximum cash offer.

A good, conservative rule of thumb is to use 40% as the normal expense ratio for property maintenance, repairs, taxes, insurance and capital replacements. Add another 10% for management, and net income can be figured to be 50% of the gross scheduled rents.

In this example, the rent for similar houses in the area is $1,200 per month. 50% of $1,200 is $600, which equals the net monthly income. To annualize the net income, multiply $600 times 12 months, or $7,200.

By dividing the $7,200 annual income by the desired return on cash investment, 8%, the maximum cash offer that can be made to purchase this property is $90,000. If a lower purchase price can be negotiated, the return on investment increases.

What about terms of sale? This means the property can be purchased for less than full price, if paid in cash, by a buyer who obtains bank-loan financing or takes title subject to an existing loan; by a seller who agrees to finance some of his or her equity; or by a combination of the above.

This is a form of financial leverage that we discussed in Chapter 13.

7. **Investment-to-value ratio** – This is the total dollar amount of cash and financing dedicated to acquiring the investment divided by the market value of the property asset.

For a simple example, if a property is purchased for $50,000 with an additional $10,000 needed for property rehab—a total investment of $60,000—and the property after rehab has a market value of

$100,000, the investment-to-value is 60%.

Adding a slight variation to that example, let's put $10,000 of our own money in the deal and use private financing of $50,000. The total of cash and financing is still $60,000, so the total investment-to-value for the buyer is 60%.

> *It is very possible that if the buyer is in default, the property condition will not be equal to the market value.*

However, for the private lender who will hold a first lien security instrument and note (meaning his $50,000 interest comes before the $10,000 down payment of the buyer), the investment-to-value ratio is only 50%.

Which position would you prefer? The answer is "it depends."

The passive private lender with a first lien security interest of $50,000 is very safe at only a 50% investment to value. If the buyer goes south and defaults on his obligations, the private lender can foreclose the buyer's interest and take over ownership of the entire $100,000 property.

It is very possible (and likely) that if the buyer is in default, the property condition will not be equal to the market value of $100,000. The passive lender-investor has a couple of options, if he or she does not want to be involved in property management or rehab.

That investor may, through his/her network, find another active partner who would be happy to take over the interest of the defaulted party for part of the cash flow and equity. Or, the passive lender may simply wholesale the property for cash to an active investor interested in a great deal on this property at $55,000 or $60,000.

In either case, the private lender can be made whole without getting his/her hands dirty dealing with property issues that he/she never wanted in the first place.

Investment-to-value is an important consideration when investing in real estate.

A good rule of thumb is to stay at or below 70% investment-to-value. There could be times when an investment with a higher investment-to-value might be within a legitimate range, and times when lower investment-to-value should be used. The investment-to-value ratio is one method for reducing risk.

CHAPTER KEY TAKEAWAYS

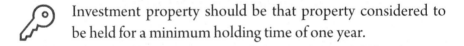

Investment property should be that property considered to be held for a minimum holding time of one year.

The chief criteria for evaluating a property are size, location, floor plan, updates, gross scheduled rent, price and/or terms, and investment-to-value ratio.

A good rule of thumb is to allocate 40% of gross scheduled rents to expenses such as insurance, taxes, maintenance and tenant turnover.

An investment property should be considered first for its ability to produce long-term stable cash flow.

NOTES

_____

_____

_____

_____

_____

_____

_____

_____

_____

PLAN OF ACTION

_____

_____

_____

_____

_____

_____

18 HARD MONEY LENDING - INVESTMENT OR BUSINESS?

HARD MONEY LENDING requires greater knowledge, has more risk, is a business and not an investment strategy. Hard money refers to the fact that the lender looks first and foremost to the collateral property as the security and not so much to the quality of credit of the borrower. As such, hard money loans can provide returns of 14-18% or more.

Besides the higher risk and need for a higher degree of active involvement, most hard money loan terms are for four to six months to one year or less. Once the loan has matured and the investor paid his principal and interest, the investor has to find another suitable loan to make and start the process all over again. Otherwise, the investor's money may sit idle for some time, earning no interest or yield. This is known as "yield drag."

On the contrary, a good property has to be purchased only once, can be held as a rental for many years, throwing off increasing cash flow via rising rents and appreciating in value. By owning a good property, you have a one-time investment risk.

Making hard money loans turning over twice a year is a lot of work (a business), with a fairly high risk that some of those loans will go bad and result in legal collection efforts and ultimately foreclosure.

Hard money lending requires greater knowledge, has more risk, is a business and not an investment strategy.

The amount of cash needed to begin a loan portfolio varies with the risk, knowledge and experience of the investor. Obviously, a small amount to invest may mean having a portfolio of a single loan, which is more risky than having more money invested in a diversified portfolio of twenty loans.

A mostly passive investor can achieve a return of 6-10% annually in private lending. A more active investor, sourcing and negotiating his or her own transactions, may earn 10 -20%.

• Hard money lending is a business and not an investment.

• Most hard money loans are relatively short-term for less than one year.

• Hard money loans provide a higher rate of return due to the risk and amount of time and due diligence required.

• In order to be involved in hard money loans, one must have a reasonable amount of   cash available to invest.

CHAPTER KEY TAKEAWAYS

Hard money lending is a business and not an investment.

Most hard money loans are relatively short-term for less than one year.

Hard money loans provide a higher rate of return due to the risk and amount of time and due diligence required.

In order to be involved in hard money loans, one must have a reasonable amount of cash available to invest.

NOTES

_____

_____

_____

_____

_____

_____

_____

_____

_____

PLAN OF ACTION

_____

_____

_____

_____

_____

_____

19 High Cash Flow Yields - Performing Notes Secured

WITHIN THE REALM of debt-secured investments, also known as "notes or mortgages," is the category of performing and non-performing notes secured by real estate.

Private mortgage lending can provide high rates of return relative to bank CDs, savings or the bond market, but no chance for appreciation and no inflation protection.

Owning income properties (equities) will provide a smaller amount of current income, but provide inflation protection, capital appreciation potential and sometimes the possibility for profit gains when purchasing at significant discounts in the market.

Ownership of real estate can also be leveraged. It is possible to acquire real estate notes with leverage, but that discussion is beyond the scope of this book.

For experienced and knowledgeable investors, some kind of split between real estate equity and note investments can make a lot of sense. Notes are ideal investment vehicles for self-directed qualified account investing which is discussed in more detail in Chapter 24.

A performing real estate note secured by real estate can be thought of as being a lender or being "the bank." Owning or holding a note receivable with specific real estate as the collateral can be an excellent source of passive cash flow income with good yields (interest rate return) and safety when purchased properly and with good due diligence of both the security (collateral property) and the borrower/payor.

In an ideal situation, the note holder investor, acting as the bank, simply receives regular checks (mailbox money) based on the terms of the investment note. Seller-financed notes, or financing carried back by the seller of property, is negotiable, or can be sold to another party or investor.

The inherent value of such a note is based on six primary criteria:

1. The borrower's credit history

2. The borrower's down payment

3. The specific collateral property – size, location, type (single-family, duplex, four-plex, mobile home on land), and condition

4. Terms of payment per the note – interest rate, amount of payment(s), interval of payments, maturity date (when the full amount is due)

5. The seasoning or history of payments made (not applicable if a new note)

6. Documentation––the completeness and legal provisions contained in the paperwork

For most seller-financed notes, not all of the above criteria will be excellent or even considered good. In fact, the very reason for seller financing is often to sell property that is, for specific reasons, difficult to sell in the conventional market place. That's why most seller-financed notes sell at a discount to the face value of the note.

In other words, a note might have a current balance of $50,000.00 with monthly payments scheduled for 10 years secured by a good condition, smaller, single-family house in a blue-collar demographic area. The market price for such a note could be a range of $35,000 - $45,000, for example, depending on the buyer's evaluation of the six criteria above. It's all about risk.

The higher the risk, the greater the discount required. By discounting the face value of the note, the investor's yield increases. Depending on the risk, yields on performing real estate secured notes today might range from 5% up to the mid or high teens.

There are further methods of both reducing investor risk and/or increasing yield by the negotiation of the purchase by the savvy investor. The investor can choose his level of comfort when investing in private mortgage notes by deciding to invest in either 1st liens or 2nd liens. 2nd liens are also called junior liens and carry more risk because they are "second" in position and security to the 1st lien note holder.

- Investing in performing real estate notes is analogous to being "the bank."

- Most seller-financed notes are sold at a discount to the face amount or principal balance owed on the note.

- The higher the risk factors, the greater the discount required when selling a note.

- Discounting a note increases the yield or interest rate return.

CHAPTER KEY TAKEAWAYS

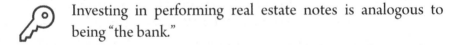 Investing in performing real estate notes is analogous to being "the bank."

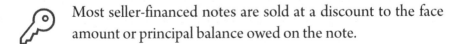 Most seller-financed notes are sold at a discount to the face amount or principal balance owed on the note.

The higher the risk factors, the greater the discount required when selling a note.

Discounting a note increases the yield or interest rate return.

NOTES

_____

_____

_____

_____

_____

_____

_____

_____

_____

PLAN OF ACTION

_____

_____

_____

_____

_____

_____

20 BACK DOOR REAL ESTATE INVEST- MENT — NON-PERFORMING NOTES SECURED BY REAL ESTATE

NON-PERFORMING NOTES ARE those real estate secured notes that are currently in default—the borrower or payor has stopped making the scheduled payments per the terms of the note. In such a case, the note holder, a bank, hedge fund, or private individual, has several options to recoup the investment.

First, it is always recommended that legal collection efforts begin immediately under the regulations of the Fair Debt Collection Act and the Dodd Frank Consumer Protection Act. Certain legal notices are delivered to the payor and if ignored or no attempt to make payment is made, foreclosure of the note and lien may ensue, allowing the note holder to take both legal title and possession of the property. The note holder can then dispose (sell) the property for cash, with financing, or keep the property.

Another option is referred to as "the workout." A note holder of a non-performing note may be able to enter into communication and negotiation with the payor and come to an agreement to modify the note terms in such a way to allow the payor the opportunity to remain as owner of the property as long as the modified terms are met.

If modification with the payor is not an option, sometimes a payor will agree to a "Deed in Lieu" of foreclosure, commonly referred to as "cash for keys." Rather than incur the legal costs and lost time of a legal foreclosure, a note holder investor might offer the payor a certain amount of cash if the payor will vacate the property, deed the property back to the investor, and provide the keys for access and possession to the note holder.

Lastly, the note holder and payor might work together on a work-out known as a "short sale." In this case, the note holder investor agrees to allow the owner/payor to market the property for sale and accept a cash offer from a third-party buyer that is less than the full amount owed on the note. Again, depending on the property location and condition, the short sale can have merits for both parties.

Because of the additional risk and potential time and legal costs involved in either a workout or eventual foreclosure of the collateral property, non-performing notes are sold in the secondary marketplace at very large discounts to the face amount of the note, often 50% or more depending on the property location and the lien position (1st or 2nd).

Because of the additional risk, non-performing notes are sold at very large discounts.

Investing in non-performing notes can be a very lucrative investment strategy for investors with experience and background in evaluating such notes and with an understanding of the workout options.

Access to banks or hedge funds that hold large quantities of performing and non-performing notes is often a barrier to entry in this investment asset class. One needs to be semi-active in order to develop the relationships necessary to gain such access.

CHAPTER KEY TAKEAWAYS

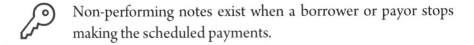 Non-performing notes exist when a borrower or payor stops making the scheduled payments.

Several options are available to the note holder in dealing with a non-performing note.

Because of the potential cost of workout, collection or foreclosure, non-performing notes sell at a very large discount to the unpaid principal balance owed on the note.

Non-performing notes can make very lucrative investment opportunities for the experienced and well-connected investor.

NOTES

_____

_____

_____

_____

_____

_____

_____

_____

_____

_____

PLAN OF ACTION

_____

_____

_____

_____

_____

_____

21   THE VELOCITY OF MONEY

A CONCEPT THAT goes hand in hand with the disciplined use of leverage is the velocity of money. Generally, when solid investment strategies are in play, turning one's investment capital over from one investment to the next, then taking the profits and investing them in the next deal is the fast track to wealth and replacement of passive cash flow for one's labor.

Once a certain magnitude of capital has been amassed, it becomes more difficult to keep a larger amount of investment capital turning as quickly as a smaller amount. In other words, the more capital one has to invest, the more difficult it is to find appropriate investments where that money can earn the higher rates of return that are possible with smaller investment amounts.

Therefore, when one has reached a certain level of capital—that number being different for everyone, depending upon lifestyle needs and replacement income needed—one would be in a position where capital preservation with less risk and less return would be the best strategy. At some point enough is enough, and there is no reason to remain as actively involved in turning one's money over as in the beginning.

For example, an entrepreneur in his or her 30s is able to save $15,000 per year to acquire interests in capital investments. Because this 30-something has energy, ambition and time, he/she can be active or, at least, semi-active in investments. Every year this person is able to find good real estate investment deals through marketing, networking and negotiation skills.

This person brings in passive capital joint-venture partners to fund the majority of the deals he/she finds, and splits the $15,000 of investment capital into three $5,000 portions that he/she allocates to three different option positions to be taken with his/her self-directed Roth IRA in other people's deals.

Our young entrepreneur is well leveraged in his/her own deals by using private lender money and with his/her own saved money in highly leveraged IRA accounts. In five years, his/her IRA options— three per year for a total of 15 options—have increased to $300,000, or a total return of more than 20% annually.

Because of the time required to fund small deals ($5,000 each), it would take 60 such deals to keep turning the $5,000 investment increments and maintain the 20% yield return rate. Instead, the young entrepreneur funds five $5,000 option deals per year, and the balance of the investment capital goes into a few larger investments, an average of $50,000 each.

At that amount, the person is investing in about 11 deals per year, which is just right for the time he/she has available to lead-generate and put together joint ventures. Instead of earning 20%-plus, these larger investments, very safe and secure, earn approximately 10% annually—still a very good return.

The point here is that those who need to build wealth quickly should use both the leverage of smaller amounts of capital and the velocity of money to turn those smaller investments and realize the profit—and then do the same thing as frequently as possible.

As the capital investment base grows significantly, a lower rate of return on deals that are longer-term, stable investments can be satisfactory for continuing wealth growth. Some of the capital can still be leveraged into smaller deals with leverage to maximize returns. Tax-deferred traditional or tax-free Roth IRAs are perfect vehicles for growing the money quickly.

CHAPTER KEY TAKEAWAYS

During wealth-building years, keeping one's investment capital moving or "turning" more frequently will allow for faster growth.

Financial leverage will allow one's investment capital to turn and grow more quickly.

Once an investment goal has been reached, the prudent investor will focus more on capital preservation and less risk with longer-term investments.

Minimizing taxes will also greatly improve overall wealth-building.

NOTES

_____

_____

_____

_____

_____

_____

_____

_____

_____

PLAN OF ACTION

_____

_____

_____

_____

_____

_____

22   WHAT'S A FAIR RETURN ON INVESTMENT

YIELD RETURNS SHARED between the active and passive investor are not set in stone. Every deal is different. The basic parameters of a deal should be considered in developing fair structures for each party:

1. 50-50 equity deal – In this scenario, the active partner finds a property, negotiates its sale, closes with the passive investor as title holder (owner) and agrees to manage the investment deal until exit (when it is ultimately sold).

The private passive-investor provides 100% of the funding to acquire and rehab the property. This is an "equity investment," whereby the passive investor who funds the deal takes title or ownership and the active managing-partner has a management contract and option for his or her interest.

The net cash flow (after all expenses) is split 50-50 between the investors. The net equity (proceeds after costs of sale less the passive investor's original investment) is also split 50-50. The passive investor always receives his or her original investment capital out of the sale proceeds before any other profit is split.

2. Debt deal – In this scenario, the active investor partner finds, negotiates and closes the deal in his own name or entity name. The passive investor funds 100% of the acquisition and rehab costs. The passive investor has a first-lien security and promissory note with stated terms, usually monthly interest.

The point here is that there are no set standards for joint venture deals.

If the passive investor wants only an interest rate return with no equity participation (inflation hedge), then a return of 5-8% interest-only paid monthly would be reasonable in today's market for a passive investor who is well-secured.

In this same example, the private investor and active partner may agree to provide the passive investor with some percentage of the equity in the property as a hedge against future inflation.

Formulas that allow different variations of this example include:

• 6% interest only paid monthly, plus 25% of the net equity when the property is sold.

• 4% interest only paid monthly, plus 50% of the net equity when the property is sold.

• 2% interest only paid monthly, plus 75% of the net equity when the property is sold.

• No payments during the holding period and 100% of the net equity when the property is sold.

Why would a passive investor not want any current cash flow and 100% of the future equity in the property? Perhaps this investor has enough active income to provide for his/her lifestyle and does not anticipate retiring from active work for a number of years. Receiving cash flow in the form of interest payments would likely be taxable to this investor at ordinary income tax rates, which might be as high as 39%.

The reduction in net income and investment growth after taxes is a given. If this investor instead takes no current cash flow (interest income) and defers all of the investment into an equity position, the investment will grow without the effect of taxes and he/she can take the profit in the future when active income is not being produced.

The point here is that there are no set standards for joint venture deals. One must assess the four parts of any deal (discussed in Chapter 14) and determine which party is responsible for each part of the deal. Additionally, the risk to each party must be assessed in terms of investment-to-value ratio and the experience and track record of the active investor.

A side note: Equity deals are generally safer for the active investor than debt-structured deals. This is because equity deals provide for a sharing of net cash flows and profits. Debt-structured deals involve a definite promise to pay—the promissory note must be paid whether the deal is providing the anticipated cash flow or not. While it is always possible to re-negotiate with a real person (as opposed to a bank) and convert a debt-structured deal to an equity deal, it is safer to start with equity deals.

Some active investors do not like equity deals because they usually give up more of their overall cash flow and equity profits to the private passive investor. This is only fair, because with the equity deal the passive investor is accepting a share of whatever the deal actually produces vs. a guaranteed payment of the return on the investment plus the eventual return of investment capital.

With a debt-structured deal, the active investor is promising a specific return to the passive investor regardless of whether the deal produces the desired cash flow and profit. This provides the passive investor with a more stable return and possibly less overall yield return than the equity deal.

Many active investors use a combination of equity and debt deals to balance the risk and profit potential in their investment portfolios. Passive investors can do the same, depending on the specifics of a deal and the joint venture partner who will be actively managing the investment deal.

CHAPTER KEY TAKEAWAYS

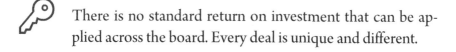

There is no standard return on investment that can be applied across the board. Every deal is unique and different.

The level of experience, risk and time will be factors in the return on investment expected by an investor.

Return on investment can be split between current income cash flow and future capital gain profits.

Equity investments are generally safer for both parties than debt-structured deals but also involve more detailed record-keeping.

NOTES

_____

_____

_____

_____

_____

_____

_____

_____

PLAN OF ACTION

_____

_____

_____

_____

_____

_____

23 DOCUMENTATION - SECURING THE DEAL

DOCUMENTS HAVE BEEN used in the United States for years to define and describe the separate interests, responsibilities, duties and obligations of any party to a real estate transaction. The purpose of this book is not to make you an expert in real estate documentation or to describe every document that might be used. Instead, here's a list to help you become familiar with the documents commonly used in single-family house investment transactions:

1. **Contract for purchase and sale** – A contract is a written agreement that provides, in this case, for the terms of sale of the real estate property. The two primary parties to this contract are the buyer and seller. Each state in the union has its own State Bar-promulgated forms that are used by licensed real estate brokers (so they can fill out forms for their clients without being accused of practicing law without a license).

As a non-licensed principal in a contract, you (buying or selling) may use any contract and language desired. But until you become versed in the basics of real estate contracts, please have a knowledgeable broker or attorney review your contracts.

2. **Warranty deed** – A document that shows the title holder or owner of the property asset.

3. **Promissory note** – A document that describes the terms of repayment of the debt on a debt-structured investment deal.

4. **Deed of trust or mortgage** – The security agreement used to tie the promissory note to the specific real estate property as collateral. Some states use a mortgage and some a deed of trust. They serve the same purpose.

5. **Joint venture agreement** – The agreement that documents the responsibilities and expectations of each joint venture party in an equity-investment deal.

6. **Management contract** – The agreement that provides for the active joint-venture partner to manage the property, locate and manage tenants, do repairs and maintenance, and provide the sharing of net income with each joint venture partner.

7. **Option** – A contract that provides the holder the right to purchase a future interest in real estate during a specified time period and for a specific price and terms.

8. **Assignment or transfer of note and lien** – This instrument transfers the rights and interest in a promissory note and the accompanying security agreement.

9. **Collateral assignment of note and lien** – This instrument allows the holder (owner) of a note and security agreement to use the existing note and security agreement as collateral for a new debt (promissory note). This means that the holder/owner of the existing note and security agreement "pledges" his/her ownership in order to borrow funds on a new promissory note with its own terms of re-

payment.

The beneficiary or lender has three levels of security protection: the person who pledges his/her interest; the maker or payor on the existing note; and the supporting collateral (property). In addition, the person pledging interest does not give control of the underlying note and security agreement. In contrast, the holder/owner of the same note could simply sell that note and security agreement to raise funds instead of borrowing (pledging) them.

Which is best? It depends on the tax consequences of pledging vs. selling; the need/desire of the potential private lender; and how much capital the owner of the note/security agreement needs to raise.

10. Release of lien – This instrument terminates the security agreement lien against a specific property when all of the terms of repayment of a promissory note have been met.

Every one of these documents may be (and should be) recorded in the county or jurisdiction where the collateral property is located (with the exception of the contract for purchase and sale, which is not usually recorded). In order for a document to be so recorded, it must be acknowledged and witnessed by a licensed notary.

The recording and filing of these instruments show the ownership of the property so that it cannot be transferred to multiple unknowing parties, which would constitute fraud.

Title insurance or third-party escrow companies provide title review services and insurance to protect the title or debt interest in a property should a defense against the title ever become a problem. When in doubt have a knowledgeable real estate attorney review all documents related to your transaction, both prior to and at the closing.

CHAPTER KEY TAKEAWAYS

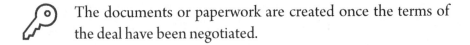 The documents or paperwork are created once the terms of the deal have been negotiated.

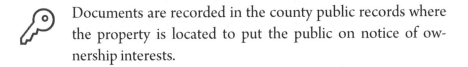 Documents are recorded in the county public records where the property is located to put the public on notice of ownership interests.

Transactions should be closed through third-party attorneys or title company offices to protect the interests of all parties.

Experienced attorneys should be used to prepare and/or review all closing documents.

NOTES

_____

_____

_____

_____

_____

_____

_____

_____

_____

PLAN OF ACTION

_____

_____

_____

_____

_____

_____

24 What's the Downside Risk?

THERE IS NO such thing as a "safe investment." Even hiding cash in a mattress or burying it in the backyard has a risk component. Most people have a problem evaluating various investments and figuring out how much risk they can tolerate.

As a long-term investment (five-10 years or more), real estate is the only asset class we know of that can and will produce a stable and predictable return, relative to other investments described in this book. Real estate provides benefits that no other investment class can. With real estate, we deal in what is called an inefficient market.

This means that no one exchange, broker or other middleman can at any time produce an exact measurement of the market value of an asset. Real estate is local, and other than mutual funds or real estate investment trusts that pool investor money, there is no way for institutions to manipulate or interfere with real estate markets like they do in the financial markets (stocks and bonds).

Gold and precious metals do have "spot market" trading values, but those assets provide no cash flows or dividends and are used only as a hedge against inflation or a total currency collapse.

By using the principles in this book, risk is greatly reduced. Always perform the appropriate due diligence on the subject property and your potential joint venture partner, and utilize the knowledge and expertise of professionals such as CPAs, brokers and attorneys to review investment transactions.

By using the principles in this book, risk is greatly reduced.

Unless you are an active and experienced investor, stay out of speculative markets in California, Florida, Arizona and Nevada, where the risks are greater.

Buying the right properties—cookie-cutter, conforming houses in good, stable neighborhoods with wide appeal for long-term cash flow and equity —is the formula that has worked well for countless investors who maintain a disciplined approach.

Avoiding the use of bank or institutional financing for the purpose of leveraging into real estate investment is fundamental.

Finally, determining the appropriate investment-to-value ratio will provide adequate margin in a falling market or in the event a joint venture partner goes completely sour and the remaining partner must foreclose on the interest of the other partner. This is rare, but it is always best to discuss and anticipate worst-case scenarios.

CHAPTER KEY TAKEAWAYS

 As a long-term investment, single-family real estate investment provides very stable and predictable investment returns.

 Focusing on the right property in the right location and with the right financing or price is the key.

 Speculation, using bank financing, or flipping properties is a business, not an investment. Never confuse the two.

 Investment-to-value ratio, or the dollars invested relative to market value, provides a margin of investment safety not available with other investment classes.

NOTES

_____

_____

_____

_____

_____

_____

_____

_____

PLAN OF ACTION

_____

_____

_____

_____

_____

_____

25 ARE THERE ANY GOOD DEALS LEFT?

SOME MIGHT ASK if all the good deals are gone. Have real estate prices already gone up too much?

Economic cycles are the investor's conundrum. When to invest and when to get out? Buy-and-hold, or try to beat the market at its own game?

Economic cycles also cause chaos and uncertainty out of which is borne the opportunity for the savvy investor.

Buy-and-hold investing has a proven track record in real estate. If one uses the criteria set out in this book to invest—with a five- to 10-year minimum investment perspective—in good, solid single-family houses in geographic areas where the economy is stable, there is no better investment for building wealth and passive cash flow.

Speculators are people who attempt to jump in and out of markets with precision timing. Sometimes it works, sometimes it doesn't. Those who continued to speculate during the previous housing bubble, created by the loose credit financing of Wall Street and pushed by politicians on both sides of the aisle, lost a lot of equity when the bubble burst.

By using the financing and disciplined leveraging techniques taught in this book, the long-term buy-and-hold investor will not be adversely affected by normal economic cycles.

Cash flow is king. Every real estate investment deal should provide sufficient cash flow from day one (or when the property is rehabbed and ready to occupy) to cover normal property expenses, management, and debt-leveraged financing—and still leave a positive cash flow of 20% or so of the gross scheduled rents.

This is the margin of safety. In the event housing values go down 15-20% in any given cycle, rents may also go down by a similar amount. With a cash-flow safety margin, the down cycle can be weathered into the next up cycle, where cash flows and equity values will trend up again.

CHAPTER KEY TAKEAWAYS

 Good deals are available in any market—you just have to know how to find them.

 Cash flow is king. Tax benefits and upside equity profit should be considered icing on the cake.

NOTES

_____

_____

_____

_____

_____

_____

_____

_____

_____

PLAN OF ACTION

_____

_____

_____

_____

_____

_____

26 Your Investment Team

KEY PEOPLE OR business services to have on hand to help you evaluate a potential real estate investment, structure the investment and close the transaction might include:

- Joint venture partner – either active or passive
- Real estate broker or agent
- CPA
- Real estate attorney
- Title or escrow closing company
- Loan servicing company
- Home inspection service
- Contractors in specialty service areas, such as plumbing and electrical

The best way to build your team is to ask. Become involved in local real estate, network and Meet-up groups. Find out who others are using on their team. Get the names of several referrals and interview them to see if there is a fit.

It is important to have team members who understand you, can work with your personality and expectations, and who will have your best interest at heart.

NOTES

_____

_____

_____

_____

_____

_____

_____

_____

_____

PLAN OF ACTION

_____

_____

_____

_____

_____

_____

.

27 401(K)s And Self-Directed IRAs, Health Savings Accounts and Coverdell Education Savings Accounts

IN CHAPTER 12 we discussed the negative impact that federal and state taxes have on the accumulation of wealth. We found that reducing the effect of taxation by 13% could increase the growth factor of an investment by a multiple of 5.

What if we could defer that tax completely during the growth phase and take distributions (cash flow) completely tax free? Remember the compounding effect of doubling a dollar each year for 20 years? The result was $1 million.

With a tax rate at 28%, the accumulation was reduced to $250,000. At a 39% tax rate the net growth was a mere $13,000. By reducing the effect of taxes on one's investment capital, compounding can grow the capital to the fullest extent possible. This is a strategy that bears serious consideration; it is worth the time and effort to learn the basics of it, in order to take advantage of the many opportunities it affords.

The ability to self-direct one's retirement account investment activities is readily available through IRS-approved third-party administrators. Some of those companies are:

Large Self-Directed IRA Custodians (more than $2 billion under custody):

Equity Trust Company

First Trust Company of Onaga

Guidant Financial (TPA)

IRA Services Trust Company

Millennium Trust Company

Pensco Trust Company (acquired Lincoln Trust Company)

Provident Trust Group

Trust Company of America

Mid-Sized Self-Directed IRA Custodians ($500 million – $2 billion)

GoldStar Trust Company

New Direction IRA (TPA)

NuView IRA (TPA)

SunWest Trust Company

Vantage IRA (TPA)

Small Self-Directed IRA Custodians (less than $500 million)

American IRA (TPA)

Quest IRA (TPA)

Kingdom Trust Company

Next Generation Trust Services (TPA)

Self Directed IRA Services, Inc. (Horizon Bank)

CamaPlan

A number of accounts can be self-directed, including 401(k)s, traditional and Roth IRAs, Health Savings Accounts and Coverdell Education Savings Accounts. The maximum annual contribution for each account type varies.

Readers of this book now understand the basic tenets of investing smaller amounts of investment capital and leveraging them into larger amounts through the velocity of money and joint venture investing.

Every application of real estate investment discussed in this book can be utilized in a self-directed account. There are rules against what is called "self-dealing," that is, using one's self-directed account to benefit the account owner individually.

This is known as a prohibited transaction. A self-directed account should be considered a different person from the beneficiary, or owner of the account, and funds and benefits cannot be mixed together.

There also are rules regarding "disqualified persons" and a self-directed account. Spouses and linear ascendants and descendants of the account holder, or beneficiary, may not participate in any investments or other dealings with the owner of the self-directed account.

Self-directed accounts are ideal vehicles for passive real estate investments similar to those discussed in this book because the owner or beneficiary of the self-directed account cannot be actively involved in the specific real estate investment.

This makes the joint venture structure ideal for these investments. An active catalyst can find and put a good investment deal together and involve a non-related party's self-directed investment capital to fund a participating interest in the investment.

Every self-directed administrator provides customer service and guidance into setting up self-directed accounts, along with education and guidance into the rules regarding prohibited transactions and disqualified persons.

CHAPTER KEY TAKEAWAYS

Reducing the effect of taxation by 13% can increase the growth of the investment by a factor of five—this is huge!

The ability to self-direct qualified retirement accounts is available through numerous IRS-approved third-party custodians throughout the U.S.

Every application of real estate investment described in this book can be done through self-directed accounts subject to IRS rules (see disqualified persons and prohibited transactions).

Debt-secured (lender) investments are ideal for self-directed accounts.

NOTES

_____

_____

_____

_____

_____

_____

_____

_____

PLAN OF ACTION

_____

_____

_____

_____

_____

_____

28   YOUR NEW PLAN FOR BUILDING WEALTH

AFTER READING THIS book, we hope you've replaced some old mindsets with new paradigms. The old-school, traditional "work hard to age 65, earn and save until you can retire" just doesn't ring true anymore; instead, the new model of "sacrifice early to leverage into capital assets that can replace your labor-produced income, providing you with security, a Plan B and peace of mind" is the way to go.

This can be accomplished by age 35 or even younger, depending on a person's lifestyle, overhead and discipline; it will take five years or fewer for those not in over their heads with education loans, consumer loans or other bad debt.

This book has covered the reasons that real estate is one of the best investments to create capital wealth and reduce the dependence on one's labor-produced income. No other investment class has all the advantages of an inefficient marketplace (where small investors have the ability to benefit without institutional manipulation).

Real estate also enjoys the opportunity to leverage, as well as the tax advantages of depreciation to offset current income, and tax-deferred exchanging to defer taxes on profit gain indefinitely.

Furthermore, for legacy and estate planning purposes, heirs to investment property receive what is called a "stepped-up basis," which means that once your property is inherited, heirs inherit title to it at a fair market value basis and can sell it and receive the proceeds essentially tax-free.

As an investment, real estate is not a "flip this house" concept.

As an investment, real estate is not a "flip this house" concept. There is the business of real estate, which has a lot of moving parts and risk, and there is the long-term investment of real estate. Unless you are or want to be an active player, real estate investment is where you want to be.

Our discussion on single-family houses revealed why this asset class is the safest and most reliable real estate investment for most investors. There are houses everywhere, and people will always want and need houses.

Good houses in good neighborhoods retain long-term stability in cash flow and value, even through the natural economic cycles that will occur.

Finally, we covered the merits of utilizing real estate as a vehicle to increase the growth and yields on retirement accounts such as 401(k)s, self-directed IRAs, Health Savings Accounts and Coverdell Education Savings Accounts, allowing for tax-deferred and tax-free distributions. Considering the effects of taxation on our investment growth, discussed in Chapter 12, this is a huge benefit.

So what's your excuse? As this book shows, limited time and money are not valid excuses for staying away from real estate.

The myth that in order to invest in residential single-family houses one must become a full-time landlord and deal with contractors and tenants is just that—a myth. Through joint-venture investment structures, you can diversify into many good investments without spending much time other than to perform due diligence on both the property and the joint venture partner.

CHAPTER KEY TAKEAWAYS

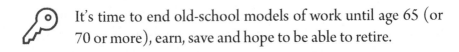 It's time to end old-school models of work until age 65 (or 70 or more), earn, save and hope to be able to retire.

Learning to acquire and leverage capital assets can create a Plan B model to reach true financial freedom by age 35.

Real estate is one of the best investments to create capital wealth and reduce dependence on one's labor-produced income.

Real estate investment can be used very effectively for estate and legacy planning.

One does not have to become a landlord or manage a contractor in order to effectively invest in real estate.

NOTES

_____

_____

_____

_____

_____

_____

_____

_____

_____

PLAN OF ACTION

_____

_____

_____

_____

_____

_____

29 Bonus Chapter
An Introduction To Syndications

As I shared earlier in this book, when I first started investing in real estate (way back in 1980 - I was still in dental school), I began by investing in single family rental homes. Over the next 20 years, my portfolio grew to contain dozens of these single family homes. At that time, single family rentals were an ideal asset class and helped me achieve my financial freedom.

So why bother with any other asset class (such as syndications provide)? For two main reasons.

First: Markets change. When single family markets are at historic highs, it becomes difficult to find acquisition opportunities that are below market premium. As markets recovered from 2008 and rose to new heights toward the end of the last decade, I took that opportunity to harvest equity gains from some of my single family properties. As markets shift and change, it is critical to adapt and take what the market gives you.

Second: Single family rentals are difficult to scale. Warren Buffet once claimed that he would gladly invest in thousands of single family homes across the US -- if he could find a way to do it feasibly. This is the simultaneous opportunity and challenge of that market. Single family rentals are such an inefficient market that it is difficult for the big players to swoop in and commoditize. This creates a big opportunity for small-time investors to create value at a hyper-local level. However, when your portfolio grows beyond 15-20 properties, it can become very difficult to manage well.

Syndications can offer strategic opportunities to deploy larger amounts of capital into real estate without having to oversee dozens of unique, individual investment properties. It offers the opportunity to focus and scale.

Those are the two key reasons I have added syndications to my portfolio - and they might be a good fit for you as well.

Within the real estate alternative investment space, funds and syndications are the two more passive investments. In this chapter we'll offer a brief overview of syndications, what advantages they offer to your portfolio and what potential challenges they may introduce.

What are Syndications?

A Syndication is an investment vehicle in which multiple investors pool their capital to invest in one single asset, managed by a project sponsor or operator, for a predetermined length of time.

It's worth noting that a syndication is different from a fund. A fund is an investment vehicle in which multiple investors pool their capital to invest in multiple assets (managed by a professional fund manager or team) - usually on an ongoing basis.

Each of these access points brings its own risks and rewards to y-our portfolio, depending on how it is structured. In this chapter, we'll be discussing syndications, specifically.

Why Invest in Syndications?

A syndication--a collaboration of many investors pooling their capital into one single asset--is a passive investment. If you were to buy a single-family home, as a direct owner, you are responsible for every clogged toilet. In contrast, a syndication is managed by a sponsor who maintains control over every aspect of the deal, from raising capital, to overseeing the value-add phase (i.e. renovations, infrastructure improvements), to executing the exit strategy. Like traditional real estate holdings, syndications share the benefit of depreciation, which can mitigate (but not always eliminate) tax consequences.

Syndications have the potential to generate strong returns based on value-add and good management. These returns come in the form of cash flow, which may include a preferred return (pref). Returns are divided between the sponsor and the investors, in what is known as the "split." A deal might be structured so that it also contains an internal rate of return hurdle (IRR hurdle). This means that the deal is structured with one set of terms, say an 8% pref and 70/30 split until you reach a 15% IRR, and then the split goes to 60/40 or 50/50.

In addition to cash flow, syndications generally expect to generate returns through appreciation that comes at the end of the deal, when the asset is sold or refinanced. During the life of the deal, you will generally have no liquidity, beyond the cash flow that is generated monthly, quarterly or annually.

As with most things in life, everything we've just described can be positive and negative, depending on the deal itself--but most importantly, on your needs as an investor. While many people relish the idea of a passive investment, the prospect of having cash flow without ever unclogging a garbage disposal again might not be enough to offset the total lack of control you have during the course of the deal. Now if you've picked a high quality sponsor, you should be able to sleep at night, knowing that your hard-earned money is in their capable hands; in fact, you're benefiting from their expertise. However, if you've cut corners in your underwriting and handed over your cash to the first sponsor (or marketer) who sent an offer of a glittery "guaranteed" return to your inbox, well, that could end up being a major, long-term drawback while your money is committed-- and totally out of your control.

The issue of commitment is a significant consideration when deciding whether to invest in a syndication: typically you put your money in a project and, until there is an exit (whether that's a partial or full sale, or refinancing), the money's stuck. A lack of liquidity is not a problem if you've allocated your assets with an eye toward future needs, anticipating the life events that can be forecasted (a grandchild headed off to college) and leaving reserves for unanticipated circumstances (an injury that pushes you into early retirement). For people who still have active income and are in a high tax bracket, a lack of liquidity may actually be a positive; if they go into a growth stage, they avoid having additional taxable income.

Then, as your cash flows in, be aware that you won't be able to reinvest your distributions in the syndication. You'll have to go reinvest it somewhere else, to keep it working for you. This is not a problem if you have a network that helps you keep your money invested, but you're still responsible for making the decision of what to do with it. The same goes for the end of the deal, when your investment becomes liquid again: Now you've got to get back to work, underwriting a new deal, if you want to continue to stay involved in the syndication space.

Finally, because a syndication is usually one single deal (versus a fund), one of the drawbacks is that it is not a vehicle for diversification. Essentially, one deal amounts to putting all those eggs in one basket. However, as long as you can contribute the minimum required amount, you can diversify by deploying your money in different syndications, as well as funds.

Due Diligence

Unfortunately, at the top end of market cycles, there are often a plethora of sponsors and marketers hawking syndication deals to inexperienced investors. Due diligence is essential. Dig deep behind the numbers promoted by the deal marketer. Look at the track record of the management team, assess the amount and type of leverage that the deal is utilizing, stress test the numbers and evaluate what happens to returns if not everything goes according to plan.

Also, consider the tax implications. When investing into a syndication from an IRA that is employing the use of leverage, you will likely incur a UDFI tax (unrelated debt finance income). We don't have time or space to evaluate all of the tax implications of investing in syndications within this chapter, so please consult your CPA or tax advisor.

Additionally, investors should carefully consider the liquidity options for investors. Many syndications offer limited liquidity options (or none at all). Be sure that investing in syndications fits within your overall investment strategy.

Conclusion

Syndications can be a viable investment vehicle for high-net worth investors who prefer to invest passively, or who have more wealth than can be easily deployed into individual single-family investment properties. Investors should carefully consider their priorities (cash flow vs future growth), diversification preferences, and do extensive due diligence on the deal sponsor and management team behind the syndication before investing.

CHAPTER KEY TAKEAWAYS

A syndication is an investment vehicle in which multiple investors pool their capital to invest in one single asset, managed by a project sponsor or operator, for a predetermined length of time.

Syndications can offer strategic opportunities to deploy larger amounts of capital into real estate without having to oversee dozens of unique, individual investment properties. They offer the opportunity to focus and scale.

Many syndications offer limited liquidity options (or none at all).

Unfortunately, at the top end of market cycles, there are often a plethora of sponsors and marketers hawking syndication deals to inexperienced investors. Due diligence is essential.

NOTES

_____

_____

_____

_____

_____

_____

_____

_____

_____

PLAN OF ACTION

_____

_____

_____

_____

_____

_____

30 Bonus Chapter True Stories Of Financial Freedom

Dr. Merril & MJ Rowe:

Dentist, Colorado

I have always been bad at investing. I found out that I had lost $2.2M the same day that my youngest son, Alex was admitted to Dartmouth, which was the school that he had set his heart on attending. And I had to come home and look at MJ and look at Alex dancing around the kitchen, and I had this huge sinking feeling in my stomach. Scary.

I first visited Freedom Founders, I listened to David and I listened to other people in the room, and I said to myself, "This makes sense." People were very welcoming. I wanted to be part of the community. I figured: "I've lost more money than this going down the wrong road, so let's give it a shot."

I fully believe that you can't figure out things entirely by yourself in this life. You need to bounce things off others: A friend or an adviser, and David became both that day. We took those steps home and we did them one by one. We checked them off, and we're achieving what we set out to achieve.

So I'm going to go out, and we're going to ski, and we're going to bike, and we're going to hike, and we're going to go places. We hope that with the transition and having more free time, we can take some bigger trips. We're able to do this because we are relatively young. The average dentist now is retiring at age 68, and I'm going to be able to do it with MJ while she's still able to do it as well. I want our kids to know that we enjoyed life. We worked hard, and we were a team together.

I want to enjoy my family, my friends. I want to enjoy this world. I want to enjoy being with MJ and doing things together. The idea of doing good works and of being part of the world at large is important.

Dr. Ben & Sondra Jensen

Dentist, South Dakota

Sondra and I have always been good at saving money, thanks to the lessons her father gave us. We never expected to make much profit when I bought a three-operatory practice in rural South Dakota. But with careful budgeting and hard work, we grew into a state-of-the-art clinic.

Our choice to practice in a rural area matched our values of being near family and having a more relaxed pace of life. Sondra is able to take care of the boys, and I don't miss any of their soccer games. But it also means that I have to think about retirement differently. In our part of the world, there isn't any security in an eventual sale of my practice.

I've always been a seeker in terms of wealth independence. Sondra and I had been in groups for real estate investors, but I was looking for something passive that would make a difference in terms of my ability to retire.

After our first weekend in Dallas, Sondra and I looked at each other. We knew we had found the right fit. Right away, Freedom Founders felt like something different. It shifted my perspective on investment 180 degrees.

It allowed me to step off the hamster wheel and take off an additional day per week. Now I go into work, and I'm excited to see my staff. We give high-fives in my office. In the last couple of months we've had two of the most productive days we've had in the whole time that I've been practicing. And we continue to have record months.

Having cash-flow has created enormous freedom for us. Money in the mailbox makes us feel more free. I had been thinking we needed to continue to plug away for the future. But now when we see the mailbox money come in, it makes that next step more realistic. Freedom Founders led the way for that. I certainly wasn't going to come to it on my own.

Dr. Raj Dhamrait

Dentist, Illinois

I've always wanted to have a plan B. Maybe it's because I'm a Capricorn, who always wants security. About five years ago, I found out through the Profitable Dentist that there was a DVD on "building your plan B." I watched it, and I was like, "Wow." At that point, I had no debt, and I had saved a lot of money. I could see the value in being in real estate, but I didn't have enough confidence to engage in anything.

I'll never forget my first meeting. It was mind blowing. I took a ton of notes. Now I've been a part of Freedom Founders for four and a half years. When I first joined, it was something that I didn't know that I was missing, but I really was missing. It's so refreshing to be in a room of like-minded dentists who sincerely want to help you. Most of us will find that in our local communities, even though we might be friends with dentists, they're not too open as far as exchanging ideas or doing a deep dive into their own financial situation. A lot of times, our dental friends back home have barriers up.

To me, freedom means being able to make choices. I started to achieve freedom a few years ago, and it changed my whole attitude towards practicing. When I knew I didn't have to, my stress levels declined. I have my 30th dental school reunion coming up in a month, and I find myself reverting back to how I was when I was younger, when I worked hard but had a carefree attitude.

Dr. John & Jeannie Harasin

Dentist, Michigan

I built a successful practice in Saginaw, Michigan through hard work. It demanded everything I had. For so long my mind was cluttered with stress, problems, and worry. I had little time to read, listen and absorb the world outside of the business of dentistry. I built a respectable investment portfolio on Wall Street and in commercial real estate. The traditional model seemed to be working. I was nearing retirement. But then... I'll never forget that fateful day in 2007 ... The market had turned.

I lost almost a third of my investment principle overnight. My hopes of retirement were crushed. It looked like I'd have to continue practicing into my 70s. That was when I walked through the doors of Freedom Founders for the first time. I was skeptical... to say the least. Three years ago my only goal was to sell the practice, get out of dentistry, and be retired.

Today, I've sold my practice. But my retirement paychecks exceed what I used to make as a dentist...

I now am financially free. I read what I want to read and listen to speakers on a variety of subjects. I have time to think. I've raised the bar and brought more intellect into my life. I golf. I travel. I spend more time with Jeannie. I now have a passion and a desire to make an impact on people's lives by helping them become financially and personally free.

I want to impart the ability to live each day to its fullest, on your terms... without the concern or worry of financial constraints. I believe that Freedom means doing what you want, when you want, with whom you want.

Without Freedom Founders… I might still be behind the chair, practicing dentistry. But not today. Today I am Free. That's my story.

Dr. Randy Cline

Dentist, North Carolina

I've always been a hard worker. I may not be the smartest person in the room, but I can work hard, and I can make things happen. I always wanted to be my own boss and create my own future.

I built my career in North Carolina, where I was born. In 2009 after the economy turned down, I bought a second practice to fill my time. I expected to finish my career doing that. But after signs of burn-out, I started looking to create passive income. I knew there would come a time when I could no longer work six days a week at the chair.

At the first meeting, I was skeptical. I thought, "This sounds great, but can it really be done?" At the second meeting, I got more comfortable, but like most dentists, I get paralysis of analysis.

The first deal is the scariest, but everyone was so willing to guide me through. By the third meeting, I did my first deal, and I realized, "Gosh, this isn't that hard." Then one deal leads to another. Now I've done multiple deals and, knock on wood, I haven't had a single one go bad.

If you want to grow, you have to expand your comfort zone. Even after three years, Freedom Founders pushes me to learn. That's what I like. I'm on a constant quest for options. It gives me a lot of freedom knowing that I can pick from different roads.

I needed someone that I trusted to tell me that I could start enjoying the fruits of my labor. I was straddling the fence: Should I keep on working or should I sell out and retire? Freedom Founders pushed me off the fence. Now, I can finally exhale. I had been holding my breath for all of these years, hoping that I would have enough. It's a tremendous load off my back to know, "Hey, I'm there." I got here sooner than I thought I would.

APPENDIX

How You Can Multiply Your Net Worth in a Post-COVID Economy

The economy runs in cycles. According to the National Bureau of Economic Research, there were 33 business cycles between 1854 and 2009, with each full cycle lasting roughly 58 months, on average. The expansion or growth part of the cycle has lasted forty months. The contraction, or recession part of the cycle has lasted eighteen months. The most recent expansion cycle has been a record 120 months, from 2010 until early 2020, when the coronavirus pandemic triggered a government-mandated shutdown.

Most people dislike change. Routine is comfortable. It doesn't require a lot of thought when life, family and work are smooth without disruption. Unfortunately, that's not how life works, and the same goes for the economy. And how the economy runs affects every man, woman and child to varying degrees.

Those who study and understand the business cycles are able to position themselves to be: 1) defensive or protective ahead of a cycle change, and at the same time, be 2) offensive or proactive to take advantage of the opportunities that every down market provides.

Let's take a look back at the most recent business cycle to understand the effects and the opportunities. 2007-2008 was the beginning of the Great Recession. The purpose of this paper is not to delve into the causes of that downturn, but to reveal how the cycle played out and how those who increased their wealth significantly were able to do so.

It is often said that a recession flushes out the excesses in a market. During the expansion phase, businesses are growing, consumers are buying and the unemployment rate is very low. The economy is said to be in a "bull market."

In a recessionary downturn, the credit financing markets tighten which means that the availability of money or loans for consumers to buy goods and services and for businesses to expand, dries up. Lenders become overly cautious in their underwriting for fear of defaults. Unfortunately, the lack of credit is often what causes defaults and so the spiral of contraction, business failures, loan defaults and unemployment rise.

Business and real estate assets are greatly affected by the availability of credit. When banks and other lending institutions are readily lending money, and at historically low interest rates, the prices of assets go up. This was the case preceding the 2008 meltdown and again, the same true up until the coronavirus pandemic caused the economic shutdown in early 2020.

As fear pervades the marketplace and credit financing begins to tighten, consumer and business confidence shrinks. There are fewer buyers who can buy (without credit financing) and those who have the capital to buy are reluctant unless the asset can be purchased at a significant discount to offset concerns about lower future valuations.

By the time Lehman Brothers failed on September 15, 2008, the Great Recession was advancing quickly. The down cycle lasted well into 2010 with the first sparks of an upturn in late 2011-2012. Lenders began opening their doors to those with good credit. Business and real estate assets had gone through a "repricing period" of about 40 months. Those who were positioned with liquid capital or access to capital began buying assets at highly discounted values.

This is where the opportunity occurs. This is where real wealth is made. Wealth isn't lost in a recession, it only changes hands. Dramatic transfers of wealth happen during every business cycle. Those who understand this phenomenon (a very small percentage) and actually take action (an even smaller percentage) are those who appear "lucky" and ride the wave of increasing asset valuations during the next business cycle expansion, which, as noted previously, lasted about ten years. This is how one can multiply net worth by working smarter, not harder.

How do you position yourself as one of the few who takes advantage of the current coronavirus recession? Below is a short list of the key components

Selection of Asset Class

Avoid the bright shiny object, or "everything is an opportunity" syndrome. Pick an asset class and stick with it. Jumping from one idea to the next is a path to nowhere. If you like business and already know a specific business sector, that may be a good point of reference. If, like me, you prefer real estate, then choose an asset class: single-family residential, multifamily, self-storage or mobile home parks as examples. There will be deal opportunities in every capital asset sector.

Market Knowledge

Once you determine the asset class, then you must gain some specific market knowledge - knowledge of both the asset class and the geographic/demographic market(s) on which you intend to focus. Speed to goal is of the essence here. Buy speed by joining association groups, masterminds and coaching in the specific sector you have chosen. Don't shortcut this and think you can figure it all out by yourself - that takes too much time and comes with too many harsh lessons that you could avoid by accessing and leveraging knowledge and experience that is already available. Pay to play as needed. Don't be stingy.

Lead Generation

Finding the potential opportunities in your chosen asset class is the next step. In marketing, we call this lead generation. Finding sellers with various motivations to sell an asset on price or terms that would be favorable to us and still solve an immediate seller's problem requires systems and multiple marketing channels.

Lead generation is not only a skill but also requires time and dedication. Once again, rather than try to do this yourself, joint venture or hire the lead generation. If you spend all of your time trying to do it yourself, you will not be able to focus on the negotiations and closing of transactions.

Deal Structure and Negotiation Skills

There is no higher direct compensation for skill than that of a good negotiator. Period. This can be learned. As you are learning, hire more experienced negotiators and either pay them hourly, or better yet, cut them in for a percentage of the deal once it goes through. This is another way to start building your network and a team that you can do business with repeatedly. Do not try to control everything by thinking that you will maximize your profits by going solo.

Instead, you will greatly diminish your opportunities because there is only one of you and you can only do and know so much.

Access to Capital/Financing

Structuring the terms of sale is always the most fun for me and where I excel. If it is not your strong point yet, I would work on this area the most. Cash or bank financing is only one layer of the onion. In down markets, creative financing comes to the forefront and putting together what we call "the capital stack" is what makes or breaks deals.

In short, you don't have to have all of the money. You only need to know how to structure the financing. The money, or terms of sale, can come from several places. Sellers who carry back some of their equity in seller financing terms. Private capital lenders. Existing financing. Cash on hand. Bank or institutional financing.

Equity vs. Debt

In an uncertain but opportunistic economic environment (in the post-recession downturn to recovery period), using equity joint ventures instead of traditional debt financing reduces risk and provides greater accessibility to private capital.

Here's why: 1) Credit financing is often scarce during recessionary downturns and not accessible for the opportunities in the market. 2) Debt financing is often considered "cheaper" financing than equity, which is generally true during economic expansions. However, in turbulent times, debt can become the ball and chain that sinks the risk-taking entrepreneur. 3) Those who have capital to invest (private parties) usually aren't interested in debt as their investment asset. They want in on "part of the deal" (see Participations below). They have an appetite for risk that they understand and want the upside that they believe that risk should afford. 4) Equity financing means that you and the capital investor "share" in both the upside and any downsides in the deal. This means that if the deal goes bad, or doesn't produce the returns or gains anticipated, you are not on the hook for making the private capital investor whole.

Your Team

● <u>Virtual Assistant</u>. This can easily be a part time hire. Do not overlook this person. They will keep you from creating a second job. My Executive Assistant, Lindsey, allows me to run fast. She keeps all of the loose ends tied together and effectively manages the minutiae, dealflow, contracts and orchestrates the rest of the team.

● <u>Title company and attorney</u>. You need legal counsel for contract review and third-party escrow and closing transactions. Get referrals from other business colleagues in your city - realtors, bankers, CPA's etc. will know who you need to know.

● <u>CPA and accounting</u>. You must have competent books and tax advice, especially if you are involving other people's money (private capital).

● <u>Manager.</u> I don't pay management companies (though many people do). I have found that it is much better to have a joint venture partner with whom I create monthly income (from the management and caretaking of the property) but who also has a small stake in the equity of the property. This takes me out of management completely which is one of the greatest obstacles that most would- be entrepreneurs never overcome.

- <u>Coach, mentor or mastermind group.</u> (see below on "trying to do it alone"). Michael Jordan had five coaches and yet he was considered the all-time best basketball player in the world. He knew that he could not do it all by himself and that he needed outside counsel, perspective and advice in the areas that he simply "could not see." I call these "blind spots." We all have them. Outside eyes and accountability is what keeps us from going off course. Invaluable. Please do not disregard investing in help.

Where People Make The Big Mistake

Trying to do it alone. Either by thinking that they can "save money" and/or "make more profit" by doing it all themselves, they become slaves to the process and eventually, something breaks and they give up the dream.

Life and wealth-building is a team sport. Learn this skill (team building and leadership) and you can do or create just about anything you can imagine or desire. Fail in this regard and you will falsely believe that people who are successful in life are simply "lucky."

Participations are the Key

This is another form of leverage. Carving out parts of a deal; a business or real estate asset so that you can "participate" in many deals. This gives you: 1) diversification into multiple deal opportunities instead of putting all your eggs in one basket. 2) This is part of the "team concept" as illustrated above.

Not only do participations allow you to be involved in multiple opportunities, it also allows you and the other participants to bring to the table the assets and skill sets that are of highest and best use. 3)

Creating a network of people with whom you can do business increases the future opportunities for all. This is multiplication of effort and resources.

Summary

The opportunity currently at hand only occurs so many times in a lifetime. This is not a time to sit back in paralysis or simply hunker down and work harder. This is the time to multiply your efforts and assets.

The business cycle is a historical fact of life. Those who learn to embrace it and optimize it to their advantage are those who create more wealth in a shorter period with less work. It is about leverage.

For me, wealth gives me options. Wealth allows me to buy time. I cannot buy back time from the past, but I can buy time today and into the future. If I rely solely on myself and don't learn the tenets of leveraging my time and skills with other people into acquiring other capital assets, then I am destined to live the life of an average person. I don't believe in being average and neither should you.

Discover Case Studies of Real Dentists who are Creating Freedom

You'll receive a book, DVD, and Special Report that share the stories of how real-life dentists "beat the system" and took control of their retirement!

In This Package You Will Discover:

★ Stories of actual practitioners who are shaving decades off of their retirement timeline.

★ Why the "4% rule" and traditional retirement planning is FAILING - and what to do instead.

★ The difference between cash flow vs accumulation strategy.

★ How to control real estate investments without the ownership headaches.

★ Why the traditional retirement model is failing practitioners, and how to adapt to a post-Wall Street investing era.

☆☆☆☆☆

I was ready to exit my practice, David helped me clarify that process.

- Dr. Ron Barnett

☆☆☆☆☆

This just gives me a lot of confidence that there is life after dentistry.

- Dr. Mike Atencio

☆☆☆☆☆

It would've taken me 7-8 yrs to get where I've come in just 4 months.

- Dr. Greg Linney

To Request Your Free Case Study Package, Go to:

www.FreedomFounders.com/CaseStudy

Made in the USA
Monee, IL
03 November 2020

46578485R00128